The Mystery Library

Fortune-Telling

Stuart A. Kallen

Alameda Free Library
1550 Oak Street
Alameda, CA 94501

**LUCENT
BOOKS**®

THOMSON

━━━✴━━━™

GALE

San Diego • Detroit • New York • San Francisco • Cleveland • New Haven, Conn. • Waterville, Maine • London • Munich

© 2004 by Lucent Books. Lucent Books is an imprint of The Gale Group, Inc.,
a division of Thomson Learning, Inc.

Lucent Books® and Thomson Learning™ are trademarks used herein under license.

For more information, contact
Lucent Books
27500 Drake Rd.
Farmington Hills, MI 48331-3535
Or you can visit our Internet site at http://www.gale.com

LIBRARY OF CONGRESS CATALOGING-IN-PUBLICATION DATA

Kallen, Stuart A., 1955–
    Fortune-Telling / by Stuart A. Kallen.
p. cm.—(The mystery library)
Summary: Presents a description and history of some of the most popular methods of
predicting the future, including astrology, palm reading, tarot cards, *I Ching,* and oracles.
Includes bibliographical references and index.
    ISBN 1-59018-289-8 (alk. paper)
    1. Fortune-telling—Juvenile literature. [1. Fortune-telling—History.] I. Title. II. Mystery
library (Lucent Books)
    BF1861.K35 2004
    133.3—dc21
                                                                            2003010726

Printed in the United States of America

Contents

Foreword

In Shakespeare's immortal play, *Hamlet*, the young Danish aristocrat Horatio has clearly been astonished and disconcerted by his encounter with a ghost-like apparition on the castle battlements. "There are more things in heaven and earth," his friend Hamlet assures him, "than are dreamt of in your philosophy."

Many people today would readily agree with Hamlet that the world and the vast universe surrounding it are teeming with wonders and oddities that remain largely outside the realm of present human knowledge or understanding. How did the universe begin? What caused the dinosaurs to become extinct? Was the lost continent of Atlantis a real place or merely legendary? Does a monstrous creature lurk beneath the surface of Scotland's Loch Ness? These are only a few of the intriguing questions that remain unanswered, despite the many great strides made by science in recent centuries.

Lucent Books' Mystery Library series is dedicated to exploring these and other perplexing, sometimes bizarre, and often disturbing or frightening wonders. Each volume in the series presents the best-known tales, incidents, and evidence surrounding the topic in question. Also included are the opinions and theories of scientists and other experts who have attempted to unravel and solve the ongoing mystery. And supplementing this information is a fulsome list of sources for further reading, providing the reader with the means to pursue the topic further.

The Mystery Library will satisfy every young reader's fascination for the unexplained. As one of history's greatest scientists, physicist Albert Einstein, put it:

The most beautiful thing we can experience is the mysterious. It is the source of all true art and science. He to whom this emotion is a stranger, who can no longer wonder and stand rapt in awe, is as good as dead: his eyes are closed.

Predicting the Future

Everyone wishes, at one time or another, to be able to predict the future. In an uncertain world, the desire to know one's fate is as natural a trait as eating or breathing. Everyone lives, as well, with the awareness that the unforeseen consequences of a routine decision made on one day can drastically affect life for months or years to come. Many people involved in car accidents lie in their hospital beds wishing they had left the house just two minutes earlier or taken an alternate route. Of course not all events people would like to be able to predict are negative. Many wonder if they will someday find romantic love, a dream job, or great riches.

For some, the inability to know the future creates a need for endless speculation, planning, anxiety, and worry. Since no amount of preparation can really control future events, however, people have long put their hopes in divination—that is, systems for predicting the future.

Methods employed today might involve consulting psychic hot lines advertised on television or reading one's horoscope on the Internet. But divination is as old as the human race. Researchers speculate that prehistoric images of animals etched and painted on the walls of caves in France seventeen thousand years ago were symbols by means of which people hoped to influence the future. These stags, bears, horses, mountain cats, and other animals depicted by anonymous ancient artists apparently were intended to bring good luck in hunts or battles.

The first hard evidence of divination appeared around five thousand years ago in Mesopotamia, located in present-day Iraq. The ancient Mesopotamian cultures of the Sumerians, Assyrians, and Babylonians developed a complex array of fortune-telling techniques that included "listening" for predictions on the winds and studying the movements of animals. One of the most popular divination methods

Some researchers believe that prehistoric peoples painted such animal images in order to influence the future.

This bronze model of a sheep's liver reveals how Mesopotamian priests interpreted the various sections of the organ for divination.

among Mesopotamian priests was the "reading" of livers from sacrificed sheep, a practice that is called hepatomancy (*hepa*, from the Latin word for liver, and *mancy*, from the Latin word for divination). These organs were studied for unusual bumps or formations that were interpreted as good or bad omens.

Since that time, cultures around the world have tried to predict the future by hundreds of means, including cromniomancy, or divination by the smell and pattern made by onion sprouts; myrmomancy, divination by watching ants eat; and even anthropomancy, divination by interpreting the organs of freshly sacrificed human beings.

These divination methods were originally linked directly to gods, goddesses, and religion, as New Age author Scott Cunningham explains in *The Art of Divination:*

The deities, it was believed, were willing to provide hints of the future if they were given the opportunity to do so. [Opportunities were] provided to them by . . . use of specific tools, which the deities manipulated to prove specific responses. The earliest diviners thought that divination revealed the will of the deities. The future, they thought, was unchangeable.[1]

Some might scoff at these primitive beliefs, but throughout the world, people continue to read horoscopes, consult tarot cards, visit palm readers, and confer with fortune-tellers. In doing so, they are hoping somehow to fulfill that ancient human longing to predict and control their future.

The Flow of Time

Belief in divination calls into question the very nature of time—if the future can be seen, it would have to somehow already exist in the present. While this is something of a brain-teaser, it is not confined to the world of card readers and astrologers.

The ancient Greek mathematician Pythagoras believed that there was one cycle of time, and it repeated itself exactly over and over. If this were true, events in the future would play out as they had in the past. The Maya peoples who ruled Mexico around the ninth century A.D. thought that this cycle of time lasted only fifty-two years. The Maya peoples believed that future events could be predicted because they would be similar, though not identical, to what had happened in the past.

The widespread use of clocks and calendars in the Middle Ages changed people's notions of time, ruling out concepts based on cycles, which in one form or another were found in most early cultures. Instead, time came to be viewed as a swift-moving river that flowed in one direction only. People were trapped in the current, could not escape, and could not turn around or go back.

In 1905, physicist Albert Einstein challenged this linear way of thinking when he published his theory of relativity in which he stated time was fluid. Einstein believed that the past, present, and future might exist all at once or in any particular order, writing that "time, with its emphasis on the now, has no meaning . . . the distinction between past, present and future is only an illusion."[2] Although Einstein had no interest in predicting the future, others have suggested that if time is fluid, it might be possible to perceive events in the future at the present moment. This concept, however, has never been scientifically proven.

Why Do People Believe?

Such theories give hope to those who believe that the future is predictable and who forget that Einstein also said, "I never think of the future. It comes soon enough."[3] People remain interested in predicting the future, however, because it is where they are going to spend the rest of their lives. While some are content to let the future simply happen to them, others try to

Albert Einstein's theory of relativity states that time is fluid, with no real distinction between past, present, and future.

shape and mold it in various ways so that their lives will be happy and prosperous. For example, someone who wants to enjoy wealth in their future can study hard and get high marks in school. This can lead to a good job that brings fulfillment and happiness. Lightning sometimes strikes, however, and tragedy, sickness, or death may lie around the next corner. With these fears haunting the subconscious thoughts of most people, there will always be a hunger for horoscopes, tarot cards, palm readers, and other methods of divination.

Some say that knowing the future is very different from being able to change or control it. This brings to light another brainteaser: If someone foresees a disaster and does something to stop it, then is not the premonition itself nullified because the predicted accident never happened? Or is the future is fixed, so that events will take place no matter what anyone does to change them? Roman author and statesman Cicero believed this and, as such, wanted no part of divination, writing in the first century B.C.:

> [It is] not even advantageous to know what's going to happen; for it's wretched for a man to be tortured [by foreknowledge] when he's powerless to do anything about it, and to lack even the . . . [comfort] of hope, which is available to all [others].[4]

Of course millions of people dispute the notion that it is possible to know about unexpected events before they happen. Instead they attribute the popularity of such things as astrology, the *I Ching*, palmistry, and tarot cards not to the supernatural but to basic human nature. As skeptic Robert Todd Carroll writes on the Tarot Cards website:

> The need to be guided, to have assistance in making decisions, to be reassured, may have . . . roots in . . . [childhood]. For, it is in childhood that one needs guidance, assistance and direction. It is in childhood that one needs to be comforted and reassured that it is acceptable to be master of your own destiny.[5]

Chapter 1

Astrology

A strology is by far the most popular method people use to peer into the future. Nearly every newspaper in the Western world features a horoscope column, and practically everyone knows his or her astrological sign. Professional and amateur astrologers cast millions of horoscopes every year, and there are more than a dozen magazines dedicated solely to astrology.

Many of the millions of people who read their horoscope look to it for daily guidance and do not question the basic principle behind astrology, which is explained by Angus Hall and Francis King in *Mysteries of Prediction:*

> Astrologers believe that planets are somehow bound up with the rhythms of human life, and that everyone and everything on earth is affected by the cosmic conditions that prevailed [in the solar system] at the time of a person's birth. Thus the planetary patterns at the moment are thought to indicate the pattern of a newborn's personality and destiny throughout the rest of life.[6]

Skeptics, however, point out that statistically one-twelfth of all people living on Earth were born under each of the twelve astrological signs; it is highly doubtful that on any given day, more than 500 million people are all going to have experiences of the same type. For this reason, many professional astrologers feel that notoriously vague newspaper columns give astrology a bad name. Instead they prefer to cast what they say are much more accurate individual horoscopes based on a person's exact time of birth. Some astrologers are leaving the prediction business entirely and instead are using their knowledge to offer individuals guidance and counseling based on their astrological charts.

Ancient Predictions

People have been casting horoscopes for centuries, and astrology is one of the oldest forms of study known to humanity. It began many thousands of years ago, when the night

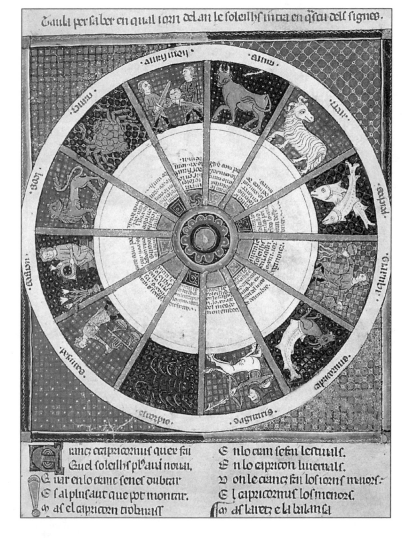

This illustration from a medieval manuscript shows the twelve astrological signs of the zodiac, with the Sun at its center.

13

Objections to Astrology

While some people believe that the movements and alignments of the planets can affect their lives, many scientists scoff at this notion. In *Objections to Astrology*, Bok and Jerome make the case that a belief in astrology is incompatible with modern science:

> In ancient times people believed the predictions and advice of astrologers because astrology was part and parcel of their magical world view. They looked upon celestial objects as [homes] or omens of the Gods and thus intimately connected with events here on earth; they had no concept of the vast distances from the earth to the planets and stars. Now that these distances can and have been calculated, we can see how infinitesimally small are the gravitational and other effects produced by the distant planets and the far more distant stars. It is simply a mistake to [imagine] that the forces exerted by stars and planets at the moment of birth can in any way shape our futures. Neither is it true that the position of distant heavenly bodies makes certain days or periods more favorable to particular kinds of actions, or that the sign under which one was born determines one's compatibility or incompatibility with other people. . . .

> One would imagine, in this day of widespread enlightenment and education, that it would be unnecessary to debunk beliefs based on magic and superstition. Yet, acceptance of astrology pervades modern society. . . .

> It should be apparent that those individuals who continue to have faith in astrology do so in spite of the fact that there is no verified scientific basis for their beliefs, and indeed that there is strong evidence to the contrary.

was lit only by campfires and people lived in small nomadic hunting tribes. The main nighttime activity for these prehistoric people consisted of closely studying the Moon, planets, and more than two thousand visible stars as they appeared to move across the sky. These observations allowed even the most primitive cultures to gain a surprisingly detailed appreciation of celestial movements. In fact, one of the oldest man-made objects ever discovered is a piece of bone with the phases of the Moon carved into it, apparently by a Cro-Magnon man more than thirty-four thousand years ago.

In the centuries since that time, people throughout China, India, Africa, the Middle East, Europe, North America, and elsewhere came to believe that the heavenly bodies, especially the Moon, the Sun, and the planets, were living gods who were responsible for all life on Earth. There was little doubt that these important cosmic deities could see into the future and reveal messages about the destiny of mortals.

These concepts were formalized in ancient Babylon and provided a foundation for astrology as it is still practiced today. Around five thousand years ago, Mesopotamian priests and magicians mapped and named stars, using the world's

This bone's markings depict the different phases of the moon, which soothsayers followed to make predictions.

first formalized system of writing, called cuneiform, which utilized more than seven hundred symbols that were carved into clay tablets. The interactions of gods and goddesses in the celestial bodies were said to influence affairs of kings, princes, and even entire nations.

For thousands of years, priests and soothsayers recorded these predictions. In a text known as *Emuna Anu Enlil*, written around 1000 B.C., the priests write that Marduk, or Jupiter, was the king of gods. When the Moon, as it orbited Earth, blocked out the sight of Jupiter, or when Jupiter seemed to disappear behind the Moon, this was taken as a bad omen:

> When the Moon occults [blocks] Jupiter . . . that year a king will die (or) an eclipse of the Moon and Sun will take place. . . . When Jupiter enters the midst of the Moon, there will be want in [the city of] Aharrû. The king of Elam will be slain with the sword: in Subarti . . . [people] will revolt. When Jupiter enters the midst of the Moon, the [prices in the markets] will be low. When Jupiter goes out from behind the Moon, there will be hostility on the land. [7]

Such dire predictions were not uncommon. However, since the Moon regularly blocks Jupiter and the ancient world constantly was marked by war, crop failures, and civil strife, soothsayers were able to compile impressive track records by announcing that certain predictable astronomical events would be followed by disaster. That the catastrophes might have had nothing to do with the alignment of the planets was a possibility the ancients do not seem to have considered.

A System Based on a Flat Earth

Whatever the predictive value of heavenly motions, ancient astrologers carefully recorded the regular changes in the positions of the planets and stars. However, they started with the false assumption that all celestial bodies, including the Sun and the Moon, revolved around Earth, which was said

The Wobbling Zodiac

The concepts of modern astrology are based on the "fixed" position of Earth and stars as they were observed more than four thousand years ago. Modern astronomers know that these reference points have changed due to a slight wobble in Earth's rotation called the "precession of the equinoxes," that has changed the seasons in relation to the stars visible in the sky. This can be seen on or about March 21, the first day of spring, or vernal equinox, marked by twelve hours of day and twelve hours of night. Twenty-five hundred years ago, when the concept of the zodiac was widely adopted, the Sun actually did rise in Aries on the first day of spring. Due to the wobble, however, the vernal equinox loses one full sign of the zodiac every 2,166 years. This resulted in the spring Sun rising in Pisces by the first century A.D. Now, in the twenty-first century, the Sun is about to enter Aquarius on the first day of spring.

(This is the source of the popular late-1960s song that cites "the dawning of the Age of Aquarius.")

The celestial slippage has caused the constellation Aries to actually be in the house of Taurus and so on, throughout the entire zodiac belt. Astrologers deal with this precession of the equinoxes in two ways. In India they acknowledge the problem and adjust their astrological readings to compensate for the reality of the shift. This school of thought is called sidereal astrology, and someone born on April 1 in India is a Pisces, not an Aries.

Most other astrologers throughout the world ignore the precession of the equinoxes. They practice what is called tropical astrology, based on the ancient perception of the stars. They believe that if they adjusted their calculations to fit with the present zodiac, it would shift everyone's astrological sign, creating cosmic chaos.

to be flat and located at the center of the universe. It is known today that the Moon is a satellite that revolves around Earth and that Earth and the planets orbit the great star of our solar system, the Sun. Ancient astrologers, however, tracked the movements of what they called the "seven planets." These were the Sun and the Moon and the true planets later named by the Romans: Mercury, Venus, Mars, Jupiter, and Saturn. (Uranus, Neptune, and Pluto cannot be seen with the naked eye and were unknown to the ancients.) In addition to the planets, forty-eight groups of stars, or constellations, which appeared to resemble animals, people, or objects, also appeared to move across the night sky at various times of the year.

In the ancient system, developed by the Babylonians around 450 B.C. and now known as the zodiac, the Sun was thought to circle Earth east to west in a 360-degree path every

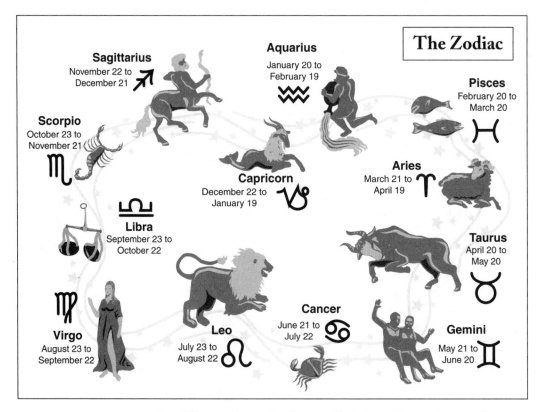

The Zodiac

Sagittarius
November 22 to
December 21

Aquarius
January 20 to
February 19

Pisces
February 20 to
March 20

Scorpio
October 23 to
November 21

Capricorn
December 22 to
January 19

Aries
March 21 to
April 19

Libra
September 23 to
October 22

Taurus
April 20 to
May 20

Cancer
June 21 to
July 22

Virgo
August 23 to
September 22

Leo
July 23 to
August 22

Gemini
May 21 to
June 20

day. This path of the Sun, called the ecliptic, lies at the center of a broad band within which the constellations also appear to travel if one observes them daily, throughout the year, from the same spot on Earth. The ecliptic is divided into twelve sections, called houses, each taking up thirty degrees. Each house contains its own constellation. Whether it is day or night, a new sign rises on the horizon every twenty-four hours, but the location in the sky changes throughout the twelve months of the year. Therefore a person facing north at midnight will see Taurus in the center of the sky in February and its opposite, Scorpio, in roughly the same place six months later in August.

The Sun rises in front of each constellation over the course of one month. For example, twenty-five hundred years ago (when the zodiac was first conceived) as the Sun rose on March 21, the first day of spring, the constellation Aries the Ram was behind it on the horizon. Thus people said that the Sun was "in" Aries. About a month later, on April 21, after "moving through" Aries, the sun appeared to be rising in front of the constellation Taurus the Bull. (These positions have changed since that time, due to an imperceptible wobble in Earth's orbit, but most astrologers continue to base their predictions on this ancient system.)

The Moon appears to travel much faster and rises in a different part of the sky—and in front of a different constellation—every two or three days. Venus and Mercury keep pace with the Sun, changing signs about once a month, while the outer planets appear to occupy the same constellation for months or even years. For example, Jupiter changes signs about every thirteen months, while Saturn takes almost three years.

Around the fifth century B.C., the ancient Greeks began to call the ecliptic the *zodiakos kyrklos,* or "circle of little animals." This was because as people looked intently at the constellations, they perceived the outlines of recognizable figures. Thus the Greeks also gave the constellations the names by which they are known today. Aries the Ram and Taurus the Bull are followed by Gemini the Twins (appears in the sky May 21 to June 21), Cancer the Crab (June 22 to July 22), Leo the Lion (July 23 to August 23), Virgo the Virgin (August 24 to September 22), Libra the Scales of Balance (September 23 to October 22), Scorpio the Scorpion (October 23 to November 22), Sagittarius the Archer (November 23 to December 21), Capricorn the Goat (December 22 to January 20), Aquarius the Water Bearer (January 21 to February 19), and Pisces the Fish (February 20 to March 20).

Casting Personal Horoscopes

In addition to naming the constellations, the Greeks removed astrology from the exclusive realm of priests and kings. Unlike the people of Babylon, who had only global predictions of the royal astrologers, average Greek citizens were able to examine their personal lives based on their horoscopes.

The methods the Greeks used to cast horoscopes have changed little over the centuries and are still in use. Today, as in ancient Greece, when a baby is born, astrologers determine the exact location of the Sun, the Moon, and the planets in relation to the zodiac at that moment. For example, if the Sun is in Leo upon the baby's birth, the child has a sun sign of Leo. The positions of the Moon and the planets are determined in the same manner, so that a child might have the Moon in Scorpio, Mercury in Virgo, Venus in Sagittarius, and so on. Another important factor used by astrologers is known as the rising sign, or ascendant. This is based on the constellation that was rising over the horizon at the moment of birth.

Spring and Summer Signs

The influence of each sign is determined by the time of year it is associated with and the entity it resembles. For example, the constellation Aries appears on the first day of spring and looks like a ram. Those whose sun sign is Aries are said to be like the spring season itself. That is, they act and think like youngsters their entire lives, are joyous like the spring flowers, and may be full of bluster like the March winds and as energetic as the ram that the stars represent. On the negative side, they may be willing to butt heads like two rams fighting or be impulsive and impatient like children. Some astrologers even believe that those born under the sign look like rams, with long noses, curly hair, and strong jaws. They point to Thomas Jefferson and Vincent van Gogh as two examples of the Arian facial type.

The influences of Taurus on a person are said to be relationed to the stoic nature of the bull seen in the constellation. People whose sun sign is Taurus are said to be patient, stubborn, down-to-earth, and slow to anger but dangerous when provoked. Because the sign appears in late April and early May, those born under the sign of Taurus are said to like bright colors like those of the flowers of spring.

Gemini people are said to have dual personalities like the twins seen in the stars. Although they are considered highly

intelligent, as if influenced by two minds, Geminis may be fickle, contradictory, or flighty.

Those born under Cancer the Crab are said to be like the oceans, feminine and receptive, but also powerful and life-giving. The masculine Leo is the opposite of Cancer. Like a roaring lion, Leos can be loud, extroverted, egotistical, and proud.

Virgos are said to embrace the qualities of the all-knowing virgin goddess that symbolizes their sign. Virgos may be wise, self-contained, critical, and analytical.

Fall and Winter Signs

Libra, the only nonhuman or nonanimal in the zodiac, is represented by the scales of balance, with a strong sense of

This eighteenth-century summer constellation chart features the astrological sign of Gemini, or the Twins.

21

justice and fairness. Scorpio appears in the fall and, like the autumn, represents life, death, and the circular march of the seasons. Those born under Scorpio can sting like the scorpion but can also be fearless, tenacious, and full of positive life energy. Sagittarius the Archer can also sting with words, but influenced as they are by the symbol of the arrow, those born under this sign are said to be travelers, friends who are straight and true, and people who can reach their goals quickly.

Capricorns, the winter sign of the Christmas season, are said to love tradition, but like the goat that represents them, they can climb steep mountains to achieve their desires.

Unlike the Capricorn, who prefers normalcy, those born under Aquarius the Water Bearer prefer to carry on with no restriction in life. Lovers of freedom, Aquarius people can follow their own paths to become great artists or musicians.

Finally, people born under Pisces the Fish, the last sign of the zodiac, are said to swim in the deep worlds of thought, imagination, and spirituality.

A Deeper Look at Pisces

While short descriptions are familiar to almost everyone, most astrologers provide much more detail for each sign, such as the following summation of Pisces by Saffi Crawford and Geraldine Sullivan in *The Power of Birthdays, Stars, & Numbers:*

> Pisceans possess a highly developed feeling nature. Sensitive Pisceans are constantly receiving impressions from their outer environment, yet they are also acutely aware of their inner prompting. They often retreat into a private dream world to enjoy the musings of their powerful, wondrous imagination and sometimes to escape the harsher realities of life. The symbol for Pisces is two fish swimming in opposite directions, indicating a dual personality of extremes. At times they can be tired and lethargic, or just drifting, and at oth-

ers they can be efficient, precise, and extremely hard-working. . . . Pisceans are very receptive to environment or the feelings of others. Combined with their remarkable imagination, this facility makes Pisceans excellent for any form of healing, music, art, drama, or photography, and particularly for things of a spiritual nature. Just as the fish swim in opposite directions, Pisceans are also open to mood swings.[8]

Such descriptions are further enhanced by astrologers in several ways. Each sign of the zodiac, for example, is said to be ruled by earth, water, fire, or air, which also purportedly have symbolic significance in a person's horoscope. For example Aries, Leo, and Sagittarius are fire signs, and fire people are said to be easily excited, impulsive, and inflammatory. On the other hand, earth signs Taurus, Virgo, and Capricorn are "down-to-earth," tending to be studious and organized.

The Sun, the Moon, and the Planets

Like the signs of the zodiac, each planet is said to have its own influence on a person throughout his or her life. For example, the Sun rules the outward personality, the Moon the inner self, Venus love, and so on. These aspects of life, in turn, are influenced by the sign under which each planet falls at any given time.

The power of each planet is not defined by appearance, as with the constellations, but by the complex mythology that originated with the ancient Greeks and Romans. For example, according to the Greeks, the Sun was ruled by the god Apollo, who traveled across the sky in his fiery chariot every day. Apollo was young, virile, and beautiful, but could turn destructive when spurned. Based on Apollo's persona, astrologers believe that a person's sun sign governs his or her spirit, will, ambition, energy, and power. Conversely the sun sign may be linked with destructive traits such as egotism, arrogance, and pomposity.

Sun sign predictions, which are said to provide a "big picture" of someone's personality, are the foundation of a horoscope. The horoscope grows in complexity, however, when the influences of the other planetary positions are added. For example, the Moon is believed by astrologers to contain the qualities of the Roman goddess Luna. Since the Moon controls the tides, the Moon's influence on a person is said to be cool, watery, and feminine, as opposed to the dry, hot, masculine Sun. The position of the Moon at birth is said to foretell a baby's future behavior with respect to his or her mother. The Moon's position also is believed to predict the side a person shows others, his or her outward personality, sensitivity, temperament, and outlook in life.

This seventeenth-century map depicts the zodiac and the planets, with Earth in the center. Astrologers believe that the planets influence personality traits.

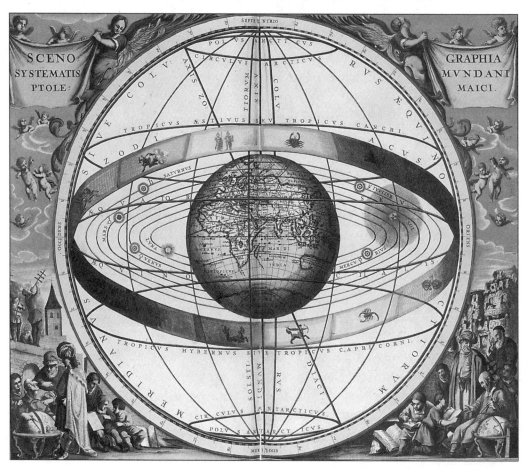

Mercury is the Roman god known as a brilliant inventor and messenger who flew through the air with a winged helmet and winged sandals. With this background, the position of Mercury in a person's horoscope is said to forecast a person's future ability to communicate, learn, and innovate as well as experience travel.

Venus, the Roman goddess of love and beauty, represents the feminine principle in a horoscope. This planet portends how a person will understand the feelings of others, express affection, and enjoy nature and art.

Mars, which reflects a red light—the color of blood—was named for the god of war: Mars to the Romans, Ares to the Greeks. The influence of Mars on a horoscope is said to embody masculine traits such as aggression, ambition, power, and action. As Crawford and Sullivan write: "Mars is the warrior god . . . [and] governs our survival instincts, whether we fight or flee. The [opposite] of Venus, Mars represents the male principle and is competitive, assertive, and ready for action."[9]

Because Jupiter was the largest planet, it was said to embody the traits of Zeus, the king of the gods in the Greek pantheon corresponding to Jupiter in the Roman pantheon. The planet therefore prognosticates how a person will be affected by religion, philosophy, justice, and spirituality.

The last of the planets known to the ancients is Saturn. As the most distant from Earth, Saturn is thought to be cold, slow moving, and large. The Greeks associated it with Cronus, the fearful chief of a race of giants called Titans. Astrologers still consider the planet's influences to be often negative and a harbinger of large events in the world, rather than individual actions.

The "New" Planets

The seven ancient planets are considered the most powerful in a person's chart. In 1781, however, English astronomer William Herschel complicated the astrologer's task by discovering Uranus, a planet beyond Saturn. Not to be undone, astrologers quickly incorporated Uranus into their calculations. Since the huge planet, which takes eighty-four years to move through the zodiac, was discovered during the time of the American Revolution, astrologers claimed that Uranus influences entire cultures and eras with disruptive changes. On a personal level, Uranus is said to govern the degree of freedom and rebellion in an individual's personality.

German astrologer Johann Gottfried Galle spotted Neptune in his telescope in 1846. Named after the Roman god of the sea, astrologers determined that this planet influenced the raw power of all humanity and the unconscious thoughts shared by all the world's citizens.

In 1930, astrolgers were once again confronted with the challenge of defining a new planet's influence on the horoscope when Pluto was discovered almost 4 billion miles from Earth. In the typically confusing language of the astrologer, Llewellyn George describes the workings of Pluto in *The New A to Z Horoscope Maker and Delineator:*

> Pluto is called masculine, stern, somewhat inscrutable. . . . Invoked by or responsive to music, especially the kind of music called jazz. Pluto rules the underworld, the subconscious workings of the body, the fluxing influences, the contest between acid and alkali; the fusing actions. [10]

The Future in the Stars?

With a baby's horoscope influenced by his or her sun sign and the position and alignment of the planets, it is easy to see how horoscopes can be individualistic. Skeptics wonder, however, how these multiple and often contradictory influences can really mean anything. In *Objections to Astrology* Bart J. Bok and Lawrence E. Jerome hypothesize that people do not really believe that the position of distant Pluto, for instance, can predetermine events in their lives. Instead the authors write that in "these uncertain times many long for the comfort of

Astrology Fails in Nepal

As the custom has been since ancient times, rulers of Nepal use astrologers to determine the timing of all important events such as marriages, elections, and business deals. In June 2001, however, Nepal's Crown Prince Dipendra went berserk and gunned down eight members of the royal family, including his parents, the king and queen, before turning the gun on himself. The prince apparently objected to the bride his parents had chosen for him. In a commentary article on the James Randi Educational Foundation website, James Randi explains that this catastrophe was not foretold by royal astrologers:

> One of the astrologers to the royal house of Nepal . . . has confessed that the recent massacre of the royal family in a hail of bullets was quite unforeseen by him and his colleagues. "No one expected it," Mangal Raj Joshi, admitted. "Heavenly planets control the situation on the ground and sometimes we are unable to explain them adequately" said Joshi, whose family has worked for more than 20 generations for the Nepalese kings. His failure—and the abject failure of astrology itself, in this catastrophic matter, has not affected his position, though. He continues as astrologer to the new monarch, King Gyanendra. His first official task for Gyanendra was to determine the most auspicious time for his crowning. We are not told if he ventured to see if flying bullets were in the new king's future.
>
> Astrologer Joshi confessed to the media that he had "lost" King Birendra's horoscope, a chart that according to the astrologer would have mapped out the dead king's life—and fate—in detail.

having guidance in making decisions. They would like to believe in a destiny predetermined by astral forces beyond their control."[11]

This longing for guidance may be reflected in the results of a 1996 Gallup poll that revealed that 100 percent of people questioned knew their astrological sign and 70 percent read their horoscopes regularly.

Whatever the statistics may say, the degree of influence of the stars and planets over a person's life is debatable. People, after all, are also strongly influenced by their parents, friends, events in their lives, and by what they see on TV. For example, two babies born at the exact same moment in the same hospital will probably lead completely different lives if one's parents are rich and the other's parents are poor. Although few would argue with this suggestion, it remains true that

Reading one's horoscope is a daily activity for many people.

many people will read detailed astrological analysis of someone they know and think it describes their friend perfectly. As Helen Gurley Brown writes in *Cosmopolitan's Guide to Fortune-Telling*, astrology "lays no claim to being rational or scientific. Quite the reverse! It aims to give you access to irrational, psychic forces that bear no relation to the laws of physics or to logical cause-and-effect. And very often, it works!"[12]

Yet even as many embraced astrology, there have always been skeptics such as the renowned Roman poet Horace, who wrote in the first century B.C.:

> Don't ask . . . what final fate the gods have given to me and you . . . and don't consult Babylonian horoscopes. How much better it is to accept whatever shall be, whether Jupiter has given many more [years] or whether this is the last one. . . . Be wise, [pour] the wine, and trim distant hope within short limits. While we're talking, grudging time will already have fled: seize the day, trusting as little as possible in tomorrow.[13]

Chapter 2

Palm Reading

Astrology relies on an understanding of complicated planetary alignment and esoteric symbolism. People who read palms, however, need nothing more than a good look at a person's hand in order to tell the future.

Palm reading, or palmistry, has been practiced since ancient times by people in Egypt, China, and India. Like many other divinatory arts, its use was often limited to religious advisers who read the palms of royalty in order to predict outcomes of wars, revolutions in progress, and other affairs of state. As happened with astrology, the ancient Greeks democratized the practice, and respected intellectuals such as the philosopher Aristotle and, later, the Roman author Pliny the Elder promoted palm reading as a valid science among the common people.

The Greeks also gave palm reading its technical name, chiromancy, which means, unsurprisingly, "telling the future from the hand." At the time the phrase was coined, palmists were concerned only with interpreting the lines that are visible on the palms and fingers. In modern times, however, palm readers also look at the size and shape of the hand and the appearance of the skin, an art called chirognomy.

The first book about palmistry, *Digby Roll*, appeared in England in 1440. This contained such dire predictions as "If there is found a line in the hill of the index [finger] . . . it tokens a person to die in a strange region, far from his own nation."[14] Thirty-five years later, another book, *The Art of Chiromancy*, was printed in Germany. These books spread the basics of palmistry among the general public and were used by those who sincerely wished to help people—and by charlatans out for easy money. Wandering families of palm readers, called Egyptians or Gypsies, attracted the scorn of religious leaders and nobility.

In 1530, Henry VIII of England enacted laws against palm reading, writing,

an outlandish people calling themselves Egyptians
. . . have . . . gone from shire to shire in great companies and used great subtle and crafty means to deceive people, bearing them in hand that they, by palmistry, could tell a men's and women's fortune, and so many times, by craft and subtlety, have deceived the people of their money. [15]

Practiced since ancient times around the world, chiromancy interprets the visible lines on hands and fingers, as shown in this sixteenth-century painting.

By the seventeenth century, palm readers were considered to be working in league with the devil and, according to historians, were associated with "thieves, rogues, and beggarly rascals."[16] At this time palmistry was outlawed in England and several other countries. By the nineteenth century, however, a revival in metaphysical belief systems such as astrology saw an increasing interest in palmistry. At that time, palmists operated on the theory that people "knew" their own future, even though many did not realize this, and that such knowledge could be accessed by means of the lines in the palms.

By 1889, palmistry was so popular that the English Chirological Society was founded in London to back claims of palmists with systematic research. Since that time, palm readers have refined their art and standardized the meaning behind the lines in the hand. Today palmistry is practiced by chiromancers who operate from storefronts, New Age bookstores, and carnival tents, as well as by amateurs who utilize knowledge about the palm from some of the dozens of books that have been written on the subject. Not everyone

The First Book on Palmistry

In 1440, an unknown author wrote *The Digby Roll Manuscript*, the first book about palmistry. The following excerpt, discussing the two longest lines that intersect in the center of the palm, was taken from the original manuscript kept in the Oxford College Library in England and published on the MS Digby Roll IV website:

First, when the line of the life and the line of the head join together in the valley of the hand, as it were against the space between the index and the mid-finger, it tokens a tendency to misfortune and wretchedness of life, sorrow of heart, and much business in gathering of possessions, and full hard to come to any thrift or to any increase of possessions.

The second, when these foresaid lines join together higher above the valley of the hand, as it were in the space against the middle of the index, it tokens subtlety of brain, ability for all manner of learning, and sharp mind and fresh of things learned and studied.

The third, when these lines are parted and dissevered above, it signifies a man that loves but himself, unwise, cruel, and envious; a back-biter, idle of words, untrue of speech, and unfaithful.

accepts the chiromantic literature as valid, as skeptic Carroll writes:

> Although you can often tell a lot about a person by examining his or her hands, there is no scientific support for the claim that you tell such things as whether you will inherit money or find your true love from the lines or marks on your hands. . . . The desire for knowledge of the future seems to be at the root of palmistry. . . . [And] fortune tellers relieve us of the obligation to gather evidence and think about that evidence. . . . They absolve us of the responsibility of decision-making. [17]

How Does Palmistry Work?

Even nonbelievers have long acknowledged that a person's personality and character may be revealed in their physical features. For example, the human face can suggest that an individual is generally mean, friendly, happy, sad, intelligent, and so on. Whether or not this is an accurate way to judge anyone, palm readers believe that the hand reveals as much about a person's character as the face.

The lines and protrusions in each human hand are unique, and to a palmist, these features can tell a story that can help someone choose a career path or make decisions about love, and they can even reveal the state of a person's health and longevity. As Sasha Fenton and Malcolm Wright explain in *Palmistry:*

> Everything about your hands, from their shape, the lines on your palms and the way you move them when talking, tells a tale about your character. Your fingernails, knuckles, and even the heel of your hand all have plenty to say to a skilled palmist. [18]

Palm readers usually observe both hands and compare the two. The dominant hand—the one a person writes with—is said to reveal individuality, choices a person has made, and how these choices will affect his or her future. The passive hand is said to show the natural abilities and personality traits a person is born with.

When practicing their art, chiromancers observe three main features of the hand: the overall shape of the palm and fingers; the fleshy parts on the outer edges of the hand, called mounts; and the lines that run through the hand.

Like other predictive arts, the four elements of earth, air, fire, and water are taken into consideration when judging the overall shape of the hand. People with long fingers, square palms, and many fine lines have air hands. These people are said to be expressive, stable, and intelligent and may be writers, teachers, or in the communications business. Those with square, deeply lined palms and short fingers have earth hands, described by Jane Struthers in *Predicting Your Future: The Complete Book of Divination:*

> This person is practical, reliable, uncomplicated, matter-of-fact and full of common sense. They are conventional and find it difficult to adapt to change. In relationships they look for a partner they can trust and who is as steady and forthright as themselves. . . . People with Earth hands often have jobs that bring them into contact with the earth or that involve hard, physical labor.[19]

Long fingers and a long rectangular palm indicate a water hand, sometimes characterized as the artist hand. People with this type of hand are said to be creative, sensitive, intellectual, and drawn to careers in fashion, interior design, or beauty salons.

Those with a long palm and short fingers possess a fire hand, which signifies an energetic, feisty, spontaneous person. According to Struthers such types "like to be in control of situations and to influence other people. . . . They are usually fit and strong, although sometimes they may eat or drink

Reading the Face

While palm reading is one of the most popular methods for predicting the future, in past centuries fortune-tellers "read" many parts of the body including freckles and moles. The art of reading facial features, called physiognomy, originated with the ancient Greeks and was very popular in the Middle Ages. The concepts behind face reading are discussed in *Charting the Future,* edited by Richard Williams:

> Seven distinct facial types were associated with the natures of the seven planets known at that time [the Sun, Moon, Mercury, Venus, Mars, Jupiter, and Saturn]. The angular, intense face of [someone such as a] soldier was linked with the forthright, martial quality of Mars. The well-proportioned, dignified, and beautiful face was seen as an expression of the creative and benign warmth of the sun. The alert, sometimes shifty face of the beggar, and the sensitive, refined face of the artist, were both associated with the planet Mercury. The round, white, bloated face, with large eyes, deeply lidded, was linked with the moon. The sallow, gaunt, ugly face, with prominent bones and stringy neck, was seen as the expression of dark Saturn. The plump face of the stereotypical well-fed priest was linked with the benevolence and cultural sophistication of Jupiter. The sensuous face of an attractive woman was a sign of the lascivious and earthy side of Venus. Such planetary stereotypes are to be found everywhere in the literature and art of the late medieval period.

too much."[20] Those with fire hands are said to enjoy risky activities, such as police work, or creative tasks in music, film, or art.

What the Fingers Show

Such general observations provide background to a palmist as he or she probes deeper into a person's character by studying the fingertips and nails. Palmists say there are four fingertip styles. Conic fingertips denote a lover of art and beauty. These graceful tips are long and narrow. Round fingertips allegedly indicate a person who is, like his or her fingers, well-rounded, or knowledgeable, and emotionally balanced. People with square fingertips are said to love order, precision, and security. The fourth type of fingertip is called spatulate, which is narrow by the knuckle but flares to a wide tip, like a rounded spatula used in cooking. When palmists observe these fingertips

The Hand of a Brutal Murderer?

In the nineteenth century, researchers studied the skulls, hands, and other body parts of convicted lawbreakers in attempts to predict criminal behavior before it happened. In *The Practice of Palmistry*, written in 1897, Comte C. de Saint-Germain claims to identify a "Brutal Murderer's Hand" and proceeds to name violent criminals whose hands reportedly had such traits:

> The great deterioration of the [Earth Hand is] manifested in the Brutal Murderer's Hand. Its characteristics may be enumerated as follows: A thick, heavy Palm, reddish in tint, and broader than the average; short awkward and stiff Fingers, generally crooked; often Spatulate . . . the second joint may be clumsy and thick; a Thumb with a "clubbed" First Phalanx [bone] and a second Phalanx very much undersized.
>
> These observations were made years ago, in the hands of Tropmann, who single-handed,

killed a family of seven people, all in half an hour. . . . [This was also seen in the hand] of Dumolard, the Lyons assassin who murdered, nobody knows how many poor servant girls; [also] of Avinain, the Parisian butcher, who killed and cut to pieces several . . . victims, and of several other infamously prominent criminals.

> It is the typical hand of the drunken brute [from] the lower classes; rarely found among educated people, no better at heart, perhaps, but craftier in the satisfying of their murderous instincts. . . .
>
> [In] this particular kind of murderer, [there is seen] the "clubbed" Thumb, the influence of which . . . causes the possessor, when his wretched, diseased nature is moved to crime to "see red" and to strike and strike his victim with blind ferocity and with sensations akin to a horrible delight.

they expect to see people who are action seekers, independent, friendly, and down-to-earth. Some people have a mix of fingertip styles, and like their hands, they are said to love diversity and to adapt easily to new situations.

Palmists use the shapes of the fingers themselves to make quick judgements about people, as seen in *The Complete Gypsy Fortune-Teller* by Kevin Martin,

> When the index finger is short, a lack of responsibility is evident. If straight, it is a sign of good character, but if crooked, it indicates a lack of self-respect. If it is very long, domineering characteristics are strong. The middle finger shows caution when long and haste when short. When crooked,

[preoccupation with unwholesome thoughts] is very evident.

The ring finger if long shows an interest only in acquiring wealth. If short, it indicates an interest in speculation and a tendency to gamble. When straight and well-formed, it shows artistic leanings, but when crooked, such talent will be used strictly for making money.

The little finger, if long, indicates that individual will do very well financially, but when it is short, he will have a much more serious struggle throughout life. If it is straight, diplomacy and taking advantage of all

Examining the shapes of his client's fingers, palms, and hand, a modern-day palmist gives a reading.

opportunities is a strong characteristic. But if it is crooked, chances in life will be overlooked, for this person will not be visionary.[21]

Palmistry and astrology have been closely linked throughout the centuries, and so the fingers themselves are named after figures in Roman mythology. The index finger is Jupiter,

A young woman offers both of her hands to be read at a Hong Kong palmistry convention.

the middle finger Saturn, the ring finger Apollo, and the little finger Mercury. These names tie the significance of the finger in palmistry with the attributes associated with the mythical personage. For example, the finger associated with Mercury the messenger indicates a person's communication skills. Thus palmists would expect someone with a long Mercury finger to be sociable, talkative, and intelligent, whereas an unusually short finger would be indicative of a person who has trouble communicating.

How each finger affects the outcome of a palm reading is governed by its length, shape, and relation to the other fingers. For example, a short Jupiter finger means a person is shy and would rather follow than lead. If the Jupiter finger is straight it is said that the person will be very observant and probably will not wear glasses. If it is crooked, the person is said to be cautious and materialistic. A long Jupiter finger shows a proud person, possibly arrogant and hungry for power. (Palmists point out that Napoléon, who conquered much of Europe in the early nineteenth century, had an abnormally long index finger.)

The thumb has its own importance to palmists, who believe that this digit reveals the most information about a person. In fact, some palmists in India need only to study the thumb to predict a person's future. According to Struthers:

> This is one of the most important elements of someone's hand, because it [predicts] their amount of willpower, the way their energies flow, their mental abilities and the strength of their character. Essentially, the weaker the thumb the weaker the person's mind and personality; and the stronger the thumb is, the more domineering and powerful the person.[22]

Palm readers look at the thumb's placement on the hand to analyze their subject's character. A thumb that is hinged low on the hand, near the wrist, is said to reveal an independent person. Like their thumb, they are flexible and easily directed. Those with a high-set thumb may be tense and introverted, especially if the digit cannot move far from the hand when pulled toward the wrist. People with thumbs in the middle are considered average and less prone to temperamental outbursts or quirky personality traits. The length and shape of the thumb is also important; according to Martin: "A long thumb shows strength of purpose, and a short one stubbornness. If straight, generosity is indicated, but if crooked only selfishness."[23]

The Mounts

The small, fleshy pads of the hand are called mounts. These are located directly below the fingers, around the sides of the hand, and above the wrist. The mounts below the fingers have names corresponding to the finger; that is, the mount of Saturn is below the middle finger, the mount of Mercury is below the little finger, and so on.

Other mounts are located in different areas of the hand. The upper mount of Mars is the pad between the little finger and the mount of Luna, which is above the wrist. The lower mount of Mars is above the thumb, and the mount of Venus is the large fleshy part of the hand below the thumb. Like every other aspect of the hand, the mounts have specific meanings and govern special parts of a person's destiny.

When reading a hand, a palmist cups the hand slightly and observes whether the mounts are large and well-defined or small and squashed in appearance. As might be expected, those with pronounced mounts are foreseen to be leaders and to be eager, energetic, and passionate. Small mounts predict the opposite, showing a person to be timid, levelheaded, and possibly a follower with little physical strength.

The meanings of the mounts generally correspond with the fingers. For example, a person with a large, well-shaped mount of Jupiter may be ambitious and destined for success; if the mount is overly large, however, these traits may be taken to the extreme by a ruthless person who does not hesitate to trample on friends as well as enemies in the pursuit of a goal.

The mounts also have relationships to others nearby on the hand. A New Age author describes the significance of the mount of Saturn, at the base of the middle finger, and what it means if it is attached to surrounding mounts:

> If the mount of Saturn . . . is non-existent, the person takes a frivolous view of life. Before reaching this conclusion, however, check that the mount hasn't merged with one of its neighbors, in which case it will blend a practical nature with ambition (Jupiter) or artistic talents (Apollo). If it is pronounced the person is studious and serious; they may also be pessimistic or fatalistic. A well-shaped mount of Saturn indicates someone who enjoys solitude and is a hard worker. [24]

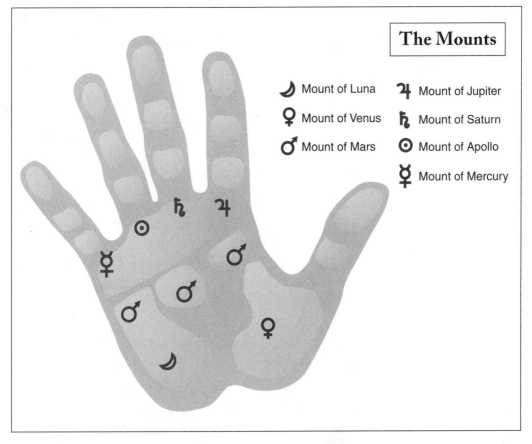

The Mounts

☽ Mount of Luna   ♃ Mount of Jupiter

♀ Mount of Venus   ♄ Mount of Saturn

♂ Mount of Mars   ☉ Mount of Apollo

                 ☿ Mount of Mercury

The mounts of Mars, characterized by the Roman god of war after which they are named, determine a person's physical and moral courage. Those with a well-developed lower mount of Mars are said to be brave and courageous. If it is overdeveloped, the person may be hot tempered, aggressive, and passionate. A weak lower mount of Mars indicates a cold person, quiet and prone to surrender when challenged.

The upper mount of Mars is indicative of moral integrity and determination. Well formed it is said to reveal a self-reliant person who possesses will power and is dedicated to his or her beliefs. If overly developed this mount could indicate a stubbornness, and problems could be foreseen because the person would tend to force his or her beliefs on others.

The mount of Luna, like the moon goddess, represents spirituality, imagination, culture, and sensitivity. The larger the mount, the greater a person's intuition and nurturing abilities. Too large, however, and the person might be a daydreamer who has difficulties functioning in the real world. An under-developed mount of Luna is said to indicate a straightforward person who has little use for fantasy in his or her life.

The mount of Venus, like its ancient Roman namesake, is about love, sensuality, and emotions. A book titled *Palmistry* describes the traits associated with a large mount of Venus:

> A large, high mount of Venus indicates tremendous sexuality. . . . A large, full Venus belongs on the hand of someone who has great energy and a desire to live life to the full. He may work hard, enjoy his sports, hobbies and interests and be enthusiastic about his family. A full Venus belongs to someone who enjoys food, drink, art, music, gardens, comfort, warmth, laughter, nice clothes and much more. He likes the company of attractive people and he gets pleasure from all manner of things that feel and smell good.[25]

A small, flat Venus mount, however, shows a person who is much more reserved in matters of love and possibly some-

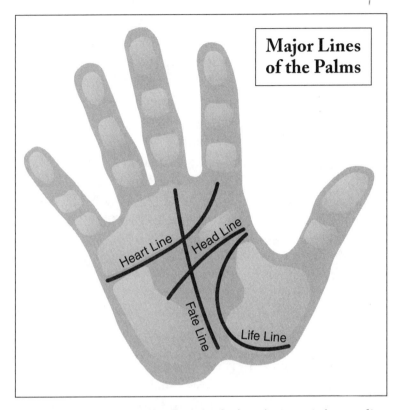

Major Lines of the Palms

Heart Line
Head Line
Fate Line
Life Line

one who is emotionally detached. A palmist might predict that such a person will have trouble developing good relationships unless they take steps to become more passionate about romance.

The Lines

Palmists believe that the mounts, fingers, and other characteristics of the hand reveal much about someone's personality and the direction their life should take. The intricate network of lines that run through the hand, however, are said to be capable of predicting a person's future. They are able to do so, palmists say, because as a person ages and matures, the lines continually change. Some lines may deepen, some may fade away, and new ones can appear in a matter of a few weeks. A contemporary expert explains the significance of the lines:

The general rule for interpreting lines is the same as for the fingers and mounts—the stronger the line, the stronger the characteristics associated with it. If most of the lines on the hand are clear and well defined but one is weak, then the energies symbolized by this line don't flow properly. People whose lines are deep and strongly marked usually achieve a lot in life. Any interruptions to the line, such as breaks, chains or minor lines running across it, indicate problems and difficulties associated with the area of life denoted by the line. In other words, the energy of that line is being diffused or interrupted. [26]

While the hand has many lines that are read by palmists, there are four major lines that are said to have the greatest importance—the life line, the head line, the heart line, and the fate line.

The Life Line and Head Line

The life line runs from the lower mount of Mars (between the thumb and index finger) around the mount of Venus to the wrist. While it is commonly believed that people with long life lines will live longer, those with short but well-marked and deep life lines can also reach old age. People with weak life lines that are feathered, marked, or broken might not live as long or might be unhealthy throughout their lives. Such beliefs have persisted for thousands of years, as Aristotle's description of the life line demonstrates:

> [The] Line of Life . . . extended to its full length, and not broken with . . . Cross Lines, [shows] long Life and Health . . . When the Stars appear in this Line it is a Significator of great Losses and Calamities: If on it there be the Figure of two O's or a Y, it threatens the Person with Blindness . . . If the Line be cut or jagged at the upper-End, it denotes much Sickness. If this Line be cut by any Lines coming from the Mount of *Venus*, it

declares the Person to be unfortunate in Love and Business also, and threatens him with sudden Death.[27]

The head line begins above the life line and moves to the center of the palm. This line determines how a person thinks and can also denote happiness in intellectual affairs. For example, a long, deep head line suggests mathematical ability and a straight, if not exciting, career path. A curving head line indicates a creative, artistic type, but a very wavy line might mean the person is subject to bouts of depression or mental illness. In centuries past, parents of a child who had many crisscrosses at the beginning of the head line might have been warned to expect trouble in school.

The Heart Line and the Fate Line

The heart line begins at the upper mount of Mercury and ends between the mounts of Jupiter and Saturn (the index and middle finger). This line is said to predict the outcome of a person's emotional and love life along with health problems associated with the heart. Like other lines, deep, long heart lines denote good things, while short, weak, or broken ones can mean trouble:

> If the line is unblemished, the subject's romantic progress through life should be straightforward. A break in the line denotes breakups in relationships and probably a broken heart. Shallow heart lines that are closer to the fingers seem to show more of these breaks and disturbances than the deeper kind of line.[28]

While affairs of the heart are important, the fate line is believed by some palmists to be the most significant line in the hand, determining success or failure in life, career, and worldly affairs.

The fate line parallels the life line by the wrist and runs toward the fingers, often ending at the head line or connecting to the middle finger. Some people have no fate line at all, but of course, a person lacking the line still has a destiny but might dislike planning ahead and prefer to let things take their own course. Strong fate lines indicate reliability, inner drive, and ambition. Breaks in the fate line can reveal changes in career, or obstacles in life.

Examining the Hand and the Self

There are dozens of other ways to read meaning into the lines of the hand. Some have physical features such as double lines, forks, splits, islands, branches, crosses, and feath-

A sign urges customers to have a palm reading to provide answers to various life questions.

ers. Interpretations are also made as to how the lines intersect with one another and with the mounts. And the lines can be used to predict the timing of events. For example, a break in the life line near the thumb is believed to indicate events that may take place when a person is twenty years old. A break near the wrist signals that the event can happen at the age of seventy.

In addition to the four main lines in the hand, there are many so-called minor lines that run around the fingers or branch off from the other lines. Chiromancers also interpret fingerprints, whorls on the palm, and even warts and blemishes. All of this complicated information can mean many different things. According to one authority: "Palmistry is a complex art. Far from the quick [inspection] of a hand, it requires an in-depth knowledge of both human nature and of the dozens and dozens of lines and symbols that may appear on the palm."[29]

A palmist's predictions, positive or negative, do not necessarily come true. The lines are always changing, however, and chiromancers believe that a person can positively control their shape and direction by assuming a better attitude or stopping negative behavior. Conversely, destructive behavior is said to reinforce negative characteristics of lines in the hand.

From one perspective, whether people's futures are written in their hands is irrelevant; it is clear, however, that those who turn to palmistry for answers are engaging in the common practice of self-examination. By studying the lines in the hand, they are probably also analyzing their own personalities as well as their jobs, friends, lovers, and other aspects of life. By trying to put their lives in perspective through palmistry, they may be unconsciously making important decisions about their own futures. And in this way palm reading can help a person to change and improve the future, as one modern author points out: "Divination isn't just about fortune-telling. It is about finding and contacting what is hidden in yourself and in the world."[30]

Chapter 3

Tarot Cards

M ost people use cards to play games like solitaire, poker, and bridge. The cards used for these games, however, are closely related to tarot cards, which have been used to predict the future since at least the eighteenth century.

Unlike astrology, which can trace its roots back to the ancient Babylonians, the origins of tarot (rhymes with "narrow") are lost to the past. Historians conjecture that playing cards originated in China around the tenth century A.D. Decks of Chinese cards were carried by traders into the Middle East and Europe around the eleventh century. At this time the cards, like those sold today, were marked by suits. They did not, however, resemble the modern card emblems of clubs, diamonds, hearts, and spades but rather utilized designs of beads, bamboo, sticks, and cups.

The Emergence of the Tarot Deck

By the fourteenth century the tarot deck emerged in Europe using several of these suits, notably sticks and cups. The tarot was similar to the standard fifty-two-card deck used today but had additional cards added for specific games. The first written evidence of the tarot came not from an enthusiast of the deck, but from Johannes of Brefeld, a monk who condemned the popular cards in 1377, calling them "the Devil's picture book."[31] The second record comes from 1415, when Filippo Maria Visconti, the duke of Milan, ordered a set of tarot cards painted by a court artist. Most researchers conclude that these cards were used by nobility to play a Renaissance-era version of bridge called "triumphs" or *tarocchi* in Italian, *tarots* in French, and *tarok* in German.

Around 1780, French spiritualists gave the individual tarot cards mystical meanings and began to use the word *cartomancy* to designate the practice of divination by cards. Once the tarot was thought of as magical tool to predict the future, believers began to embellish the history of the deck to

THE HIGH PRIESTESS.

Readers have used tarot cards like this one to predict the future since the eighteenth century.

49

make it appear more esoteric and mystical. In *The Encyclopedia of the Tarot* Stuart Kaplan cites an example:

> In 1781 . . . [French scholar Antoine] Court de Gebelin advanced the theory that the [tarot] cards constituted the Egyptian hieroglyphic Book of Thoth, saved from the ruins of burning Egyptian temples thousands of years ago. The Book of Thoth . . . allegedly contained the synthesis of all human knowledge and profound mysticism. Thoth was the Egyptian god of wisdom, occult arts and sciences. . . . Thoth's duties were to measure time and foretell the future.[32]

Since that time, other authors have falsely attributed the tarot's origins to a number of esoteric sources including ancient mystical teachings of Jews, Hindus, Buddhists, and others. In addition, people over the years have added extra meanings to each card, assigning them symbols of the zodiac or one of the four elements of air, earth, fire, and water.

Cards for Playing or Divination?

Historians speculate that tarot cards were simply used for playing card games long before they took on a mystical significance. Tom Tadfor Little explains on the *The Hermitage*, a tarot history website:

> Some time in the first half of the fifteenth century, somewhere in northern Italy, someone created the first set of tarot cards. . . . The tarot cards were used to play a new type of card game, similar to bridge, but with 21 of the special cards serving as permanent trumps [a suit in a card game that outranks all other suits

for the duration of a hand] which could be played regardless of what suit was led, and outranked all the ordinary cards. This Game of Triumphs, as it was called, became extraordinarily popular, particularly among the upper classes, and spread through northern Italy and eastern France. As the game spread to new locales, changes were often made in the pictures, and also in the ranking of the trumps, which usually bore no numbers. In time, tarot spread south to Sicily and north to Austria, Germany, and the Low Countries [the Netherlands, Luxembourg, and Belgium].

A fortune-teller creates a tarot card spread to receive answers to questions she asked while shuffling the deck.

Throwing the Tarot

In order to predict the future by means of the tarot, the cards must be laid out in a preset pattern called a spread. This can be done by the questioner, or querant, or by an amateur or professional card reader called a cartomancer.

Divining the meaning of the tarot cards is a complicated process, however. When a tarot reading is performed, the questioner shuffles the deck while concentrating on his or her problem or question. The individual, or a cartomancer, then lays out the cards one by one, or "throws the tarot." The spread determines where each card goes and what each card represents. For example someone throwing the three-card spread would lay three tarot cards out left to right. The first card symbolizes the past, the second the present, the third the future.

The simple cross spread uses five cards laid out in a cross pattern, three cards up and one on each side. The first, the bottom card, symbolizes the past and its influence on the present. The second card is laid to the left above the first. This stands for obstacles in front of the questioner. The third card is laid above and to the right of the first. This symbolizes helpful influences behind the questioner. The fourth card is in the center above the rest, standing for influences that hover above the questioner in the near future. The fifth card is in the center of the other four and represents the distant future that all other cards will influence. The sixth card of the simple cross spread is placed off to the right side. This card represents the "outcome" of the reading. The card may have a positive or negative meaning: peace and prosperity, perhaps, or betrayal and death.

More Complex Spreads

Other spreads grow in complexity as more cards are added. The ten-card spread, for example, has positions that represent the questioner's inner emotions, the immediate influence on his or her life, recent past events, goals and destiny, and other situations.

Such readings are done to predict the immediate future. Those who wish to determine events in the coming year may lay out a twelve-card spread, with each position representing a month in the year that lies ahead.

The most elaborate spread is the big-wheel spread that lays ten three-card spreads, each group representing some part of the questioner's life. For example, one position of three cards determines the past, present, and future situation of the questioner's family and domestic life. Another performs the same service concerning the specific things the questioner needs to know.

The Major Arcana

Each card of the tarot deck tells its own story and can tell the questioner his or her fortune. Copies of the duke of Milan's *tarocchi* deck have been reproduced for centuries, and the symbolism of the 1400s is still seen in tarot cards today.

Unlike playing cards that have fifty-two cards, the tarot originated as two decks that together total seventy-eight cards. One deck consists of twenty-two cards called the Major Arcana ("Arcana" is Latin for mysterious, or secret). Each card in the Major Arcana has a number, picture, and name. The pictures are symbolic and represent different parts of life and human nature.

Major Arcana cards such as Strength, Justice, and Judgment have a direct meaning. For example, if the Strength card appears in the spread of a person who wants to see into the

Major Arcana tarot cards such as Strength and Justice have unambiguous meanings.

future, the usual interpretation cites a need to be strong in an approaching situation.

Cards such as the Fool, the Empress, the Lovers, the Hermit, and the Magician represent personalities typically associated with these roles. For example, the Magician means a spiritual person is about to enter the questioner's life or that the questioner is like a magician in that he or she is self-reliant, creative, and powerful. (None of the Major Arcana cards are found in a regular deck of playing cards except the Fool, represented by the Joker, a card that usually goes unused.)

Other Major Arcana cards, such as the Moon, the Stars, the Wheel of Fortune, the Sun, and the World, deal with

Though troubling at first sight, the Death and Devil tarot cards do not necessarily spell physical death or danger.

XIII La Mort   XIII La Morte

XIII Death

XIII Der Tod   XIII La Muerte

XV Le Diable   XV Il Diavolo

XV The Devil

XV Der Teufel   XV El Diablo

broad life-changing concepts such as destiny, fulfillment, and enlightenment. In *An Illustrated Guide to the Tarot*, the Wheel of Fortune is said to be "an indicator of a stroke of luck that will leave you astonished. . . . When this arrives in a reading, fate takes a hand in your affairs and improves your fortunes, usually quite suddenly and unexpectedly."[33]

Several of the cards are traditionally associated with bad omens. Cards such as the Devil and Death can cause alarm and even terror. The Tower is another frightening card, with a picture of a tower hit by lightning and exploding in flames as people fall to their deaths. Like all tarot cards, however, these negative cards do not necessarily mean impending doom. For example, the Tower is said to show that just as lightning strikes suddenly, change can often come quickly and unexpectedly. Whether the change is good or bad depends on other factors in a person's life.

The same is true with the Death card, which does not automatically signal actual physical death. Roberta Peters, who has twenty-five years of tarot reading experience, elaborates on this theme in *Elementary Tarot*. She writes that although "hearing of a death or going to a funeral is always a possibility when the [Death card appears in a spread], the usual scenario is that some aspect of your life is about to die off and that it will shortly be replaced by something new. Very often the change is welcome. If you are hanging on hoping to resurrect something, this card tells you that you must put it behind you and move on."[34]

As with all the other cards in the Major Arcana, Death and the Devil are said to represent what renowned psychologist Carl Jung called archetypes—that is, basic symbols that have had emblematic meanings in most cultures throughout history.

Whatever the case, the cards have been designed to encompass all aspects of life, some of which can be unpleasant. A tarot authority reminds his readers that one "should note that Tarot cards, like most other forms of divinatory tools, [tend] to focus on drama, or at least strong emotions, in the life of the person whom [one] is reading for. This drama may have happened in the past, be occurring now, or will occur in the future." [35]

The Minor Arcana

Like the Major Arcana, the fifty-six cards of the Minor Arcana contain both positive and negative symbolism. They do not, however, represent broad concepts or dramatic situations. The author of *Learning the Tarot* clarifies this distinction:

> While the major arcana expresses universal themes, the minor arcana brings those themes down to the practical arena to show how they operate in daily events. The minor arcana cards represent the concerns, activities, and emotions that make up the dramas of our everyday lives. [36]

The Minor Arcana resembles a regular deck of playing cards, with an ace and cards numbered two through ten. Instead of containing a standard jack, queen, and king, however, the tarot has four so-called face, or court, cards consisting of a page, a knight, a queen, and a king. The four suits are also represented differently, with cups taking the place of hearts, swords replacing spades, pentacles for diamonds, and wands or rods for clubs.

The suits were originally believed to represent the four main segments of medieval European society, with cups symbolizing the clergy; swords soldiers, nobility, and aristocracy; wands peasants, workers, and lower classes; and pentacles shopkeepers, craftsmen, and businessmen. The suits also have divinatory meanings, with wands presaging news,

Cards of the Major Arcana

Each card of the tarot has several basic specific meanings. Below are the cards of the Major Arcana, their numbers in the deck, and what each card means, excerpted from Stuart Kaplan in the *Hanson-Roberts Tarot Deck:*

0. The Fool: Thoughtlessness, extravagance, foolishness, delirium.

I. The Magician: Originality, creativity, self-reliance, ability to accomplish a task.

II. The High Priestess: Wisdom, sound judgment, serenity, intuition.

III. The Empress: Fruitfulness, fertility, mother, sister, wife, marriage, ability to motivate others.

IV. The Emperor: Worldly power, accomplishment, wealth, authority, confidence, husband, brother, father.

V. The Pope or Hierophant: Rituals, mercy, forgiveness, compassion, servitude.

VI. The Lovers: Love, beauty, harmony, perfection, trust, honor, beginning of a romance.

VII. The Chariot: Trouble, adversity, conflicting influence, vengeance.

VIII. Fortitude or Strength: Courage, energy, resolution of problems, action, zeal.

IX. The Hermit: Wisdom, prudence, discretion, self-denial, withdrawal, loneliness, solicitude.

X. The Wheel of Fortune: Destiny, beginnings, fate, nearing the end of a problem; good or bad depending on other cards in the reading.

XI. Justice: Fairness, balance, harmony, virtue, satisfactory outcome.

XII. The Hanged Man: Transition, change, events in suspension, dullness, boredom, abandonment, rebirth.

XIII. Death: Not necessarily physical death but the clearing away of the old, unexpected loss, failure, abrupt changes, end of a love or friendship, loss of money.

XIV. Temperance: Moderation, patience, frugality, accomplishment through self-denial, successful match, good omen.

XV. The Devil: Bondage, hatred, malevolence, downfall, subservience, black magic, violence, shock, self-destruction, bizarre experiences.

XVI. The Tower: Sudden breakdown of the old order, end of a love or friendship, unexpected changes, adversity.

XVII. The Star: Hope, faith, inspiration, optimism, insight, promising opportunity.

XVIII. The Moon: Deception, obscurity, disillusionment, insincerity, disgrace, slander.

XIX. The Sun: Satisfaction, accomplishment, success, love, joy, devotion, engagement, marriage, pleasure.

XX. Judgment: Atonement, need to repent, forgiveness, rebirth, immortality, legal judgment.

XXI. The World: Completion, perfection, happy results, success, triumph in undertakings, rewards, eternal life.

Reine des Coupes   Regina di Coppe

Queen of Cups

Kelche-Königin   Reina de Copas

swords unhappiness and death, cups happiness, and pentacles money and material well-being.

Interpreting the Minor Arcana

Today the meaning of the suits has been updated to fit in with modern concepts. For example, the cups suit now signifies love and relationships, by suggesting a cup full of joy. Swords, like a sword fight, represent conflict in a person's life. Wands continue to represent jobs, careers, goals, and ambitions, but now have the supernatural association of the magic wand. Pentacles, shaped like gold coins, still signify money and material well-being.

While each suit has a broad meaning, each number within a suit has its own specific association. For example the twos represent personal power, the threes leadership, the fours excitement, and the fives competition. Thus the five of wands can be interpreted as predicting a challenge in the workplace, while the five of cups indicates an unsuccessful competition associated with love or relationships. A five of swords means opposition and severe challenges in life, while the five of pentacles stands for poverty or loss of money.

The court cards take on the traits typically associated with the archetypes depicted. For example, the king represents a mature, masculine man in the querant's future, someone who

The two kings of these cards hold in their hands symbols of very different temperaments. The sword represents a man of action and decisiveness, while the cup signifies an artistic, sensitive nature.

KING of SWORDS.

KING of CUPS.

will show authority. The king of swords is said to foretell a judicious, possibly military man, while the king of cups is associated with an artistic, educated person.

Queens are graceful, loving, mature, and feminine. When the queen of cups appears in a spread, she is a harbinger of prosperity, luxury, and charitable giving, while the queen of wands represents a sympathetic, gracious, and understanding woman in the questioner's future. As Joan Bunning writes: "A Queen is less concerned with results than with the enjoyment of just being in the world. She is associated with feelings, relationships, and self-expression."[37]

Knights symbolize impulsive teenagers who represent extremes and excess, but also sincerity. For example the knight of swords can foreshadow the influence of a brave and courageous person in the querant's life but may also predict an impetuous person rushing into the unknown, perhaps even starting a major conflict by accident.

Finally, the page is the playful child in the deck, who, according to Bunning, is acting "out the qualities of his suit with pleasure and abandon. . . . He is a symbol of adventure and possibility."[38]

Symbols of Energy

Card reading is further complicated because tarot cards, unlike playing cards, have a top and a bottom; that is, the pictures and letters on the cards are either upside down or right side up. Cards mean one thing when they fall upright and have the opposite meaning when they are upside-down, or as card readers say, reversed. For example the king of pentacles represents a man who is practical, financially comfortable, and slow to anger. If the card is reversed in a spread, it is said to symbolize a man who is corrupt and cannot be trusted, a gambler who will always seek revenge when wronged.

On the other hand, cards that represent bad omens when upright acquire positive connotations when reversed. For example the Devil card is an unpleasant sight for any ques-

THE DEVIL.

The appearance of the Devil card can represent temptation, destructive consequences, or addictions.

tioner, as it represents temptation, lust, addictions, and destructive consequences. When it is reversed, however, the news is better, as one expert writes: "The tyranny of the Devil begins to crumble. . . . The bonds that once held you so tightly are . . . beginning to slacken enough to remind you what freedom feels like. In [the reversed] position the card may

Tarot Reading for Actress Jennifer Aniston

Devotees of the tarot sometimes attempt to validate the predictive value of the practice by performing a reading for a celebrity whose lifestyle and accomplishments are well-known. Actress Jennifer Aniston, who plays Rachel on the pop-

A tarot reading for Jennifer Aniston revealed that the actress should expect a setback in her future.

ular TV series *Friends*, was the subject of one such reading. The outcome of the spread called the Celtic Cross was revealed on the *Facade* website.

The [first] card . . . represents the atmosphere surrounding the central issue. Queen of [Wands]: A person of sunny disposition, accomplished, graceful and gracious . . .

The [second] card . . . represents the obstacle. . . . Queen of Coins: A person who embodies richness and fertility, generous, opulent, gracious and noble . . .

The [third] card . . . represents your goal. . . . Seven of Cups (Temptation): Living in a world of fantasy and illusion . . . Dependence on external and even supernatural aid . . .

The [fourth] card . . . represents an approaching influence or something to be embraced. Six of Coins (Success) . . . reversed: Refusal to help others. Pomposity. Stinginess . . .

The [fifth] card . . . represents your environment and the people you are interacting with. Three of Cups (Abundance) . . . reversed: Superficial pleasure. Excessive emotion . . .

The [last] card . . . represents the ultimate outcome should you continue on this course. The Chariot . . . reversed: Bullying. Grandstanding. Sword rattling. A setback or defeat.

The reading appears to say that Aniston is a gracious person but another gracious person stands in her way. Her goals are unrealistic, stinginess is in her future, she lives in a world of superficial pleasure, and she will suffer a setback in the future.

indicate the overcoming of bad habits, destructive thought patterns, and addiction."[39]

While there is an obvious randomness as to the position of reversed cards in the deck, practitioners believe that the energy of the questioner aligns the cards and determines the outcome of the reading. Questioners are instructed along the following lines:

> Each tarot card symbolizes a particular energy, and a tarot reading shows the [combined] energies that make up a situation. When you do a reading, your actions and intentions align the energies of the moment with the cards to form a picture. . . .
>
> When a card is upright, its energy is free to manifest. Its qualities are available and active. When a card is reversed, its energy is not fully developed. It may be in its early stages, or losing power. It may be incomplete or unavailable. [40]

Does the Tarot Really Work?

Skeptics of such explanations question how a deck of tarot cards can accurately predict a person's future. An experienced tarot reader suggests that if a questioner seeks an answer to a problem, the tarot reading may help put the dilemma in perspective and help him or her focus on a solution:

> When a . . . person asks me to give an explanation of why the cards work, I usually shrug my shoulders and leave it at that. It is easy to say that the [figures] on the cards resonate with our unconscious minds, but this begs the question of why certain cards emerge in order to tell their tale. My reasoning is that a person seeking a Tarot reading is himself guided by spiritual forces to seek such a reading. [41]

While believers say that the cards can help people guide their lives, others consider them to be useful for nothing more than amusing people at parties. Even a skeptic like Robert Todd Carroll, however, believes there is a natural appeal to the tarot system:

> There is a romantic irresistibility to the notion of shuffling the cards and casting one's fate, to putting one's cards on the table for all to see, to drawing into the unknown, to having one's life laid out and explained by strangers who have the gift of [predicting the future]. . . . The idea of staring at a picture card and letting it reveal the future or mirror the soul is not one that austere critics are likely to find tantalizing, but the thought of such visionary mysticism obviously has its attraction.
>
> Some of the Tarot cards are very pretty and many of those who use them swear that they have come to a deeper and greater understanding of themselves by letting the cards stimulate their imagination. It helps them produce a [story] which gives sense, direction, and meaning to their lives.[42]

Used by 20 Million People

Ever since the first known tarot deck was produced more than five hundred years ago, card artists have faithfully retained the original symbolism of the cards while adding their own designs and interpretations. Today there are hundreds of types of tarot decks to choose from. Some have even been painted by famous artists such as Salvador Dali, others by anonymous card designers. The original fifteenth-century design has been replaced by thematic cards featuring fairies, angels, dragons, cats, and even characters from the fantasy tale *The Lord of the Rings*. Other decks are based on Native American, African, or Chinese symbolism.

Whatever images appear on the cards, their purpose is the same—to help guide questioners on a path into the future—

A tarot reader in Santiago, Chile, arranges the cards for a client. Throughout the world, tarot reading remains one of the most popular forms of fortune-telling.

and the popularity of the tarot continues to grow. More than 20 million people own tarot decks in the United States alone. Whether or not they predict the future, the cards have provided countless hours of study, fascination, and amusement.

Chapter 4

The *I Ching*

Many forms of divination that are popular today, from tarot to astrology, were also practiced in different forms by people in China. One of the most popular methods of predicting the future, the *I Ching* or *Book of Changes,* has been in use in China for nearly four thousand years and has gained worldwide popularity in recent decades.

The *I Ching* (pronounced "ee jing") is the oldest divinatory book in the world. Believers say that its contents were originally written on the back of a sacred tortoise and revealed to the Emperor Fu Hsi by the gods and spirits. For thousands of years it has been a respected source of insight into the future. Stephen Karcher, an authority on the ancient text, writes, "It was used by everyone in traditional China, from government officials to street-corner diviners. [Words] from the *I Ching* were the basis for poetry, philosophy, magic, and popular literature." [43]

The *Book of Changes* underwent several revisions as the centuries passed. Many of its passages were clarified by the son of a king in the twelfth century B.C. Around the sixth century B.C., Chinese philosopher Confucius added explanatory notes, edited the book, and reverently described it, writing:

> *The Changes* disclose things, complete affairs, and encompass all ways on earth—this and nothing else. . . . The holy sages used them to penetrate all wills on earth and to determine all fields of action on earth, and to settle all doubts on earth. [44]

By the third century A.D., the *I Ching* had evolved into something more than a book that could "disclose things." At that time a Chinese sage named Wang Bi added commentary to the book that imparted moral lessons and cosmic wisdom. That is, in addition to revealing what events would come to pass, now the *I Ching* could also point out a moral path the questioner could take in order to become responsible for his or her own future.

Although this insight was considered of manifest importance in Asian cultures, people in the West knew little

The Chinese philosopher Confucius edited the divinatory I Ching *around the sixth century B.C.*

Throwing the *I Ching* with Yarrow Stalks

In *The Elements of the I Ching* Stephen Karcher shows that the traditional method of using yarrow stalks to cast the *I Ching* is difficult and time-consuming:

- Put the bunch of 50 yarrow-stalks on the table. . . . Take one stalk and put it aside. This is the Observer or Witness. It will remain unused through the entire process of forming a hexagram.

- Divide the remaining bunch into two random portions.

- Take one stalk from the pile on your left. Put it between the fourth and fifth fingers of your left hand.

- Pick the pile on the right up in your left hand, and count it out with your right hand in groups of four, laying them out clearly on the table. Count out the sticks until you have a remainder of 4, 3, 2, or 1. You must have a remainder.

- Put this remainder between the third and fourth fingers of your left hand.

- Take the remaining pile and count it out in groups of four, until you have a remainder of 4, 3, 2, or 1. Lay the groups out clearly on the table. Put the remainder between the second and third fingers of your left hand.

- Take all the stalks from between your fingers and lay them aside. They are out for this round.

- Make one bunch of the stalks that remai[n] and repeat the procedure. Again, put th[e] stalks between your fingers aside at the en[d] of the process.

- Repeat the process a third time. This tim[e] count the number of groups of four left o[n] the table in front of you. This number shoul[d] be 6, 7, 8, or 9. It indicates the first or bot[-] tom line of your hexagram.

- To get your hexagram, repeat this proces[s] five more times, building the hexagram fro[m] the bottom up.

A diviner uses the traditional method of casting yarrow sticks to throw the I Ching.

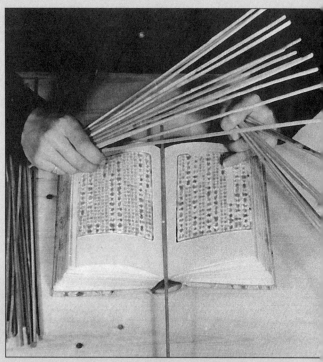

of the *I Ching* until 1882 when British scholar James Legge translated it into English. Legge's limited knowledge of ancient Chinese provided a flawed version, but in the 1920s, German missionary Richard Wilhelm translated the book into German. This version, translated into many other languages including English, is still in use today.

Throwing the *I Ching*

Blending as it does ancient Chinese mysticism with philosophies such as Buddhism and Confucianism, the *I Ching* is filled with puzzling symbolism and hidden meanings that can be even more esoteric than other divination methods. The *I Ching* "is a whole system of philosophy," the authors of the *Mysteries of Prediction* explain. "It is based on a code that embodies the traditional moral and mystical beliefs of the Chinese. Therefore, a querant cannot go frivolously to the *Book of Changes*. Nor will he or she get a direct 'yes' or 'no' answer. Questioners are thrown back on themselves for the interpretations of the answers, which are intended only as a guideline." [45]

The heart of the *I Ching* consists of sixty-four simple six-line columns called hexagrams. Each hexagram has a name, number, and written description that symbolizes a human trait or situation in life. For example, Hexagram 11 is *Tai,* or Peace, described in the *I Ching* as "Heaven and Earth interact perfectly, and the myriad things go smoothly." [46] The message of Hexagram 42, *Yi,* or Increase, is "If you are aware of the need to consider others' requirements, you can now successfully engage in bold enterprises and make major changes in your life." [47]

A questioner wishing to determine the proper hexagram for a given situation must start by formulating a question, such as "What is in the future of my career?" It is then necessary to cast a hexagram, or "throw the *I Ching*." This is done in one of two ways. The ancient method involves using a bundle of fifty dried stalks from the yarrow plant which must be painstakingly separated into several piles and counted out six times to produce numbers that correspond with lines used to form a hexagram. This process is quite complicated and can take more than an hour to perform.

Around the twelfth century A.D., the yarrow stalks were replaced with three Chinese copper coins, blank on one side, inscribed with characters on the other, and produced with square holes in the center. Replicas of these coins are still manufactured today for throwing the *I Ching*. It is not necessary to use such coins, however, and many questioners use three pennies, nickels, dimes, or any other coins.

To identify the appropriate hexagram, questioners throw the coins like dice. The "heads" side of the coin is given the numerical value of 3, the "tails" side 2. The coins are shaken and tossed on a table or floor, and their values are added up. For example, two heads and a tail equal 8. Three tails equal 6, three heads 9. (There are four possible combinations per throw, and the totals must always add up to 6, 7, 8, or 9.) The number is written down on a sheet of paper, and the coins are tossed five more times. The total of each toss is written above the one that preceeded it.

Making a Hexagram

Next to every odd number the questioner draws a solid line. Next to each even number, two dashes, called a broken line, are drawn. For example, six coin tosses that produced the numbers 9, 7, 7, 6, 8, and 9 would result in a column with three solid lines on the bottom, then two broken lines, and a solid line on top. Mathematically, the questioner can arrive at sixty-four different combinations of these solid and broken lines, and these compact little diagrams are the hexagrams of the *I Ching*.

After arriving at a hexagram, the querant turns to the *I Ching* to find the matching diagram and attempts to decipher the meaning. The hexagram corresponding to a throw of 9, 7, 7, 6, 8, and 9 is 26, *Daxu,* or Great Domestication. The

I Ching Hexagrams

UPPER TRIGRAMS

	Heaven	Earth	Thunder	Mist	Mountain	Wood	Fire	Steam
Heaven	1	11	34	5	26	9	14	43
Earth	12	2	16	8	23	20	35	45
Thunder	25	24	51	3	27	42	21	17
Mist	6	7	40	29	4	59	64	47
Mountain	33	15	62	39	52	53	56	31
Wood	44	46	32	48	18	57	50	28
Fire	13	36	55	63	22	37	30	49
Steam	10	19	54	60	41	61	38	58

LOWER TRIGRAMS

interpretation of this, like many other hexagrams, is loosely based on its appearance. For example, in this case the three solid lines represent the sky or heaven, and the hollow in the two broken lines signifies a home, while the solid line on top is the roof. As such, the *I Ching* says this hexagram represents a heavenly home "located within the Mountain: this constitutes the image of Great Domestication. In the same way, the noble man acquires much knowledge of things said and done in the past and so [brings under control and gathers] his own virtue."[48] This typically broad message is focused somewhat by Karcher, who says that it tells the questioner to gather "all the different parts of yourself and all your many encounters. Take the long view. Think of yourself as raising animals, growing crops or bringing up children. Tolerate and nourish things. Develop an atmosphere in which things can grow. Putting your ideas to the trial brings profit and insight."[49]

Yin and Yang

While there is a message contained in every hexagram, meaning has also been given to each of the six lines that make up the hexagram. Overall the lines represent the ancient Chinese concept of yin and yang. Broken lines are yin, known as fem-

The ancient yin and yang symbol represents the complementary cosmic forces that govern the universe.

inine principle, while the solid lines represent yang, or the male principle. The traditional symbol for this pair of ideas is a circle consisting of a dark half (yin) and a light half (yang). The halves, points out one source,

> are intertwined, symbolizing how interrelated and interdependent yin and yang are. In the center of each half is a small or dark seed. It is the combination of the two forces that creates a whole: one is not complete without the other. However, the forces of yin and yang are not regarded as [opposite]. They are constantly drawn towards each other and for a time they merge and then separate again. [50]

Another way to think of the relationship between yin and yang is associate them with man and woman, husband and wife. Other concepts that apply to yin and yang are soft and hard, body and mind, negative and positive. Sages in China believe that all experiences and all occurrences are a result of interaction between yin and yang. This is represented in the hexagrams, each one of which has varying degrees of yin and yang. The hexagrams, with sixty-four combinations of yin and yang lines, are said to signify all activity and transformation in the universe. This completeness, in turn, allows the hexagrams to be used in divination: by offering a symbolic representation of the forces believed to be at work in a questioner's life, the lines enable the questioner or another interpreter to formulate advice relevant to the specific situation.

The Lines

Beyond the yin and yang, the six lines of each hexagram have other, separate meanings. Each hexagram can also be seen as two three-line figures, called trigrams. There are a total of eight individual trigrams that are all possible three-line combinations of three broken lines and three solid lines. From the various arrangements of the trigrams come the sixty-four hexagrams of the *I Ching*.

The symbolism in the *I Ching* relies heavily on the concept of heaven above, earth below, or sky above and earth below. The trigrams fit into this theme by representing different aspects of this idea. For example, three solid lines means the sky or heaven, three broken lines mean earth. The other six trigrams fit into this air-earth symbolism, with air trigrams named thunder, fire, mist, and earth trigrams represented by stream, mountain, and wood. These symbols are associated with actions the questioner should take: heaven is associated with persisting; earth means yielding; thunder equals stirring up; stream symbolizes venturing or falling; mountain means stopping; wood symbolizes entering; fire, congregating; and mist, stimulating.

To apply this symbolism in analyzing the two trigrams that make up a hexagram, the *I Ching* summarizes the top and bottom trigrams in terms of "above" (and "in front") and "below" (and "behind"). For example, the trigrams of Hexagram 10, Treading, are seen as follows: "Above is Heaven, and Below is Lake."[51]

Beyond the Trigrams

Beyond the trigrams each individual line in a hexagram has its own meaning and its own significance when taken in relation to the lines around it. Each line tells a part of the story that, when taken together, constitutes the meaning of the hexagram. For example, Hexagram 10, Treading, tells the questioner that they should continue walking on the path they are on, but they may be walking a dangerous path that they share with the vicious tiger. They can take power, wisdom, and strength from the tiger, clearly a positive choice, or make it angry, which would result in negative omens.

In a line-by-line description of Hexagram 10, the first (bottom) yang line tells the questioner to tread lightly; the second line, also yang, advises that the path is level and smooth; the third line, a yin, offers this advice: "The one-eyed man may still see, and the lame may still tread, but when

A questioner throws three coins into the air. The I Ching *helps decipher the meaning behind how the coins land.*

one treads on the tiger's tail, it will bite him and he will have misfortune." The fourth line, another yang, continues the story: "One who treads on the tiger's tail here should be fearfully cautious, so that in the end he will have good fortune." The fifth line, yang again, says: "Practice constancy in the face of trouble." And the top line, also yang, warns "One should look where he has trodden and examine the omens

The *I Ching* for Rosie O'Donnell

In modern times computers have been put into service to generate readings. The *Facade* website has cast the *I Ching* for various celebrities, including Britney Spears, Leonardo DiCaprio, and Nicole Kidman. The following *I Ching* reading, for Rosie O'Donnell, seems to say that the comedian and TV personality is successful and will know joy in her future:

> The present is embodied in Hexagram 32 - Heng *(Duration)*: Successful progress and no error is indicated, but the advantage will come from being firm and correct. Any movement in any direction whatever will be advantageous.
>
> The second line, [yin], shows all occasion for repentance disappearing.
>
> The fifth line, [yin], shows its subject continuously maintaining the virtue indicated by it. In a wife this will be fortunate, in a husband, evil.
>
> The situation is shifting, but neither Yin (the passive feminine force) nor Yang (the active masculine force) is gaining ground.
>
> The future is embodied in Hexagram 31 - Hsien *(Influence)*: On the fulfillment of the conditions implied here, there will be a free course and success. Its advantage will depend on being firm and correct, as in marrying a young lady. There will be good fortune.

The things most apparent, those above and in front, are embodied by the upper trigram Chen *(Thunder)*, which is transforming into Tui *(Lake)*. As part of this process, movement, initiative, and action are giving way to joy, pleasure, and attraction.

Comedian Rosie O'Donnell will have a happy future, according to an I Ching *reading.*

involved. Here the cycle starts back, so it means fundamental good fortune."[52]

Some hexagrams are further complicated by the the fact that any yin lines derived from the number 6 or yang lines from 9 represent "moving" lines that are in the process of turning into their opposite meaning. This is based on the ancient Chinese notion that the entire universe and all human affairs are constantly changing and shifting from one extreme to another. In practical matters, a broken 6 line can be transformed into a solid 9 line and vice versa, creating an entirely new hexagram to instruct the questioner.

However the lines are interpreted, believers say that the lines within the hexagram interact with one another, as fluid as the universe, as Wang Bi wrote in the third century:

> [Distant] lines and [adjacent] lines pursue each other; lines that attract and lines that repel provoke each other; and lines that indicate contraction and lines that indicate expansion induce each other to action. . . . This is why . . . [the hexagram lines] perfectly [emulate] the transformations of Heaven and Earth and so . . . [follow] every twist and turn in the myriad of things and so [deal] with them without omission. . . . There are only one yin line and one yang line, but they are inexhaustible. [53]

How Does the *I Ching* Work?

For all their vagueness, the hexagrams in the *I Ching* are said to work like other systems of divination. That is, the *I Ching* functions as a way for questioners to get perspective on their lives and use advice from the reading to confront their problems. In this way, people can use the sometimes obscure wisdom of the hexagrams to help them to chart a course for their own future. In explaining how this works, Karcher focuses on the spirits, which are thought by some to actively participate in the reading:

> Think about it this way. You want to do something and make plans. Then you feel strange and uneasy; you sense there is something going on. You need to know what the [spirits] think about what you want to do. You want to know whether the time is right

to do it, and what sort of attitude or strategy would be most effective. Those . . . spirits . . . can either help you or seriously interfere with you. They know about things you are not aware of because they are where all your stories, images, motivations and desires come from. They can warn you, redirect you, encourage you, give you instructions on how to go about things, or forecast disaster. The [*I Ching*] opens the dialogue with these spirits, and the result of that dialogue is what the old shamans called . . . "bright spirit" . . . "clear-seeing" or "the light of the gods". It is an awareness of the [path] or way. [54]

While believers feel that the *I Ching* can show them the proper path to follow in life, skeptics think that the messages within the book are so esoteric and contradictory that they have no real meaning. As such, they cannot be proved or disproved but are simply used to confirm whatever the questioner wants to believe. For example, Hexagram 26, Great Accumulating, says "Not eating at home brings good fortune." Does this mean that good luck comes to those who eat in restaurants? Or does it mean that one should not eat in order to have a positive outcome? The meaning of lines within the hexagram further clouds the issue.

Critics also note that those who wish to discover the application of the hexagram to the situation at hand must be able to tease out logical relationships among dozens of seemingly random variables. Depending on the quality of the interpretation and the seriousness of the questioner, the results may prove helpful; or they may simply confirm whatever the questioner wants to believe.

Finally, there is the randomness of the way the hexagrams are created by throwing coins. As Robert Todd Carroll writes:

It is not too difficult to understand why ancient peoples would look to random coin tosses . . . to help them decide what to do next with their lives. They had no science, little knowledge of the nature of things, and not much more to guide them in this life than their own limited experiences and the teachings of superstitious mythmakers and storytellers. It is not

A Malaysian I Ching *reader sits ready to cast the divinatory yarrow sticks.*

too difficult to imagine why the mythmakers would come up with such methods of divination . . . if you are clever and vague enough, you can gain a reputation for wisdom and it can be difficult to prove you wrong. [55]

Whether or not one believes in the validity of a book filled with sometimes baffling ancient Chinese philosophy, the *I Ching* remains popular throughout Asia, Europe, and North America. While some believe it acts as a road map to the future, others simply appreciate it for its poetic language and timeless wisdom. Karcher puts this in perspective, writing: "You can't use it to control other people or change the weather. You can use it to become aware of and act in harmony with those . . . that you meet in your dreams every night. It can make you happier, more effective, more compassionate and more imaginative. . . . In the long run, it can change the way you see the world." [56]

Chapter 5

Oracles

Most methods for divining the future use sets of specific information that are recognized as beyond human control. Astrologers, for example, base their predictions on actual astronomical data. Cartomancers use tarot cards, with their ancient symbols, and *I Ching* readers use the sixty-four unchanging hexagrams. These predictive methods can be studied and perfected by almost anyone who can memorize the elements of esoteric systems and acquire facility in interpreting the symbols involved. One category of fortune-telling, however, does not involve cards or Chinese hexagrams, but rather relies on the alleged ability of a single person to see into the future. This person, who claims to deliver prophecies about the future, is often called an oracle, from the Latin *orare*, "to speak." Other names used for oracles include clairvoyant, prophet, seer, shaman, and soothsayer.

Long before people gathered in ancient cities to form the first civilizations, tribal shamans utilized dreams, visions, and hallucinations induced by drugs, fasting, or frenzied dancing to predict the outcomes of hunting expeditions and wars. By the time ancient Babylon was settled (around 3000 B.C.), professional soothsayers spouted prophecies that were said to be messages personally delivered to them by the gods. While these oracles gave utmost importance to dreams and visions, they also relied on a host of divinatory systems, from reading the entrails of sacrificed animals to listening for voices on the wind. These holy seers often cloaked their predictions in language incomprehensible to ordinary people. This use of ambiguous wording allowed the seer to persuade someone who had suffered because of a decision based on a prophecy that the person's interpretation had been wrong, not the prophet himself. As noted in *Premonitions: A Leap into the Future:*

> The poetic and symbolic speech of the oracles often led simple-minded kings into trouble in ancient times, when they would base the wrong conclusion on the sometimes equivocal verse of the seers . . . the cloudy language of prophesy has frequently been misinterpreted. [57]

By the time the ancient Egyptians were building the Great Pyramid at Giza (around 2500 B.C.), virtual armies of soothsayers were assigned to interpret the divinatory messages in the dreams of kings and queens. The Bible mentions one such prophet, Joseph, who interpreted a dream of an Egyptian ruler to mean that there would be seven years of prosperity and seven years of famine, events that did come to pass.

The Bible has dozens of stories of prophets who were able to predict the future after talking to God or having God-inspired dreams. In 800 B.C., a shepherd named Amos predicted that the people of Israel would be enslaved and taken to Assyria, an event that actually took place in 721 B.C. Other biblical prophets, such as Jeremiah and Ezekiel, made accurate predictions. The stories, however, were written down well after the actual events, leaving some to wonder whether the predictions might have been "backdated"; that is, credited to one of the prophets after the event, not before it.

The Oracle of Delphi

By the age of ancient Greece, kings, queens, and average citizens went to elaborate shrines, also called oracles, to speak directly to the gods about the future. At one time there were thousands of oracles found throughout Greece, and the ruins of some are major tourist attractions today. The ruins of the Temple of Apollo on Mount Parnassus at Delphi, home

Check-Out Receipt

Alameda Free Library
Main Branch
1550 Oak Street
Alameda, CA 94501
Tel: 510-747-7777
www.alamedafree.org
Checkout Date: 12-12-2014 - 14:36:20

Patron ID.: xxxxxxxxxx1904

- -

1 Fortune-telling /
33341007062473   DueDate: 01/02/15

- -

Total Items: 1

Balance Due: $ 2.40

Libraries now closing at 5:00 p.m.
on Thursdays.

We Appreciate Your Business

18921

st famous. This
housand years,
ury A.D.

ntain cave, the
tue of Apollo.
een picked by
it or died, an-
icle was named
crown, Pythia
d she was act-
ias were beau-
ter a sex scan-

*According to the Bible,
the ancient oracle and
prophet Jeremiah made
accurate predictions.*

dal rocked Delphi, the age was raised to fifty and only women
from unknown families were appointed.)

In the fourth century B.C., Greek historian Herodotus claimed that volcanic gases, emitted from cracks in the cave floor, had hallucinogenic effects on the women playing Pythia. It is not known where Herodotus acquired this information, and the truth of this assertion has been disputed over the centuries. In 2001, however, a study by a team of geologists uncovered traces of a volcanic gas called ethylene, which has a sweet smell and produces a narcotic effect described as a float-

This ancient Greek painting depicts Pythia, the Oracle of Delphi, prophesying the future to a king.

ing or disembodied euphoria. Combined with the expectations of seekers, this toxic gas may have been responsible for nearly ten centuries of prophecy.

Seekers of Delphic Wisdom

Whatever the cause of the prophecies, the Delphic oracles attracted kings, queens, and generals from many nations as well as average citizens, some of whom had traveled to Delphi from hundreds of miles away. Before seeing the oracle, these seekers performed purification ceremonies and sacrificed animals such as bulls and goats. What followed was described in the second century A.D. by Apollonius of Tyana, who descended into the cave that smelled of a

> wonderfully sweet perfume . . . [and] whose walls are decorated with the rich offerings which attest the truth of the oracles and the gratitude of those consultants who have been favored by fate. At first we had difficulty in seeing anything, the burning incense and other perfumes filled the place with dense smoke. Behind the statue of the god is the crypt, into which one descends by a gradual slope, but the servants of the temple keep the consultants far enough away from the Pythia to make their presence unnoticeable. . . . [Pythia's] chest swelled; first she flushed, then paled; her limbs trembled convulsively and more and more violently. Her eyes seemed to flash fire; she foamed at the mouth; her hair stood on end. Then . . . she uttered a few words, which the priests at her side noted down.[58]

Apollonius had asked Pythia if his name would go down in history. She affirmed that it indeed would, but it would be associated with false statements and malicious slander. This prediction came true: Apollonius was respected in his lifetime, but after his death he was maligned by early Christians. Their criticism—that he was merely a worker of illusions whose alleged magical powers were bogus—were taken to be false and slanderous by his supporters.

Like all seekers at Delphi, Apollonius was required to pay two day's wages and also make offerings to the oracle. At its height, these gifts made the shrine one of the richest in the world. The author of *They Foresaw the Future* gives examples, suggesting the extent of the wealth of the Delphic oracle:

> [Kings] and princes and humble folk came from far and near . . . with the common hope that their problems would be solved and their future foretold. They brought an increase in trade . . . but the [shrine] received the chief benefits. . . . The wealth and the [objects of art] amassed at Delphi were fabulous. In its temples and theater were golden and marble statues, whose number grew with the fame and prosperity of the place—carvings, jewels, paintings . . . , golden cups and platters, everything that symbolized opulence was to be found there.[59]

These riches reflected the belief of the donors that the predictions handed down by Pythia had been accurate. Even the philosopher Cicero, who was a skeptic about fortune-telling, had to admit that "the oracle of Delphi [never could] have been so overwhelmed with so many important offerings from monarch and nations if all the ages had not proved the truth of its oracles."[60]

While Delphi attracted the richest people, other Greek oracles were more inclusive. At the Temple of Zeus in Dodona, citizens wrote questions that could be answered "yes" or "no" on thin lead strips that were placed in a jar. A priestess oracle read them one by one and doled out answers. Many of these strips have survived. Most ask timeless questions such as "when should I marry" and "will my farm be successful."

The Oracle from France

By the time Christianity was well established in Greece, around the fifth century A.D., the oracles fell out of favor.

The Oracle Predicts Victory

The Oracle of Delphi was often used by leaders in ancient Greece to make important decisions about war. In *Premonitions: A Leap into the Future,* Herbert B. Greenhouse describes a famous incident:

> Never were . . . the other Greek city-states in greater danger than when Xerxes, the ruler of Persia, decided to invade Greece with his awesome army, the largest and most formidable in the world, in 480 B.C. . . .
>
> As the Persian armies and fleet advanced west, the Greek leaders rushed in consternation to the Delphic oracle and asked what they should do. The oracle, too, was awed by the size of the Persian forces and in twelve lines of rambling verse, suggested that . . . retreat was the only sensible course.
>
> But then the [oracle] seemed to reverse herself and said, "Truly a day will come when you will meet him [the foe] face to face." The oracle added, enigmatically, that the Greeks would find their safety only in "houses of wood" and closed with this cryptic two-line prophecy:
>
> > Divine Salamis, you will bring death to women's sons
> >
> > When the corn is scattered or the harvest gathered in.
>
> According to the Greek historian Herodotus, "The professional interpreters understood these lines to mean that if they prepared to fight at sea, they would be beaten at Salamis [a seaport]." One of the Greek leaders, Themistocles, demurred. He thought that "houses of wood" referred to ships and that the Greeks would win the war at sea. . . . The Greek leaders were won over by Themistocles' argument, and instead of a wholesale retreat, they readied their fleet for the battle at Salamis. Although the gigantic army of Xerxes swept over the combined armies of the Greek city-states, the smaller but more skillful Greek fleet overcame the Persian fleet at Salamis. This led to the defeat and withdrawal of the Persians from Greece.

Coincidentally, this occurred at a time when the gases at Delphi seemed to have weakened through lack of volcanic activity. More than ten centuries would pass before another oracle, Michel de Nostredame, startled the world with eerie predictions.

Nostredame, known as Nostradamus, was born in France in 1503. He studied math and astrology but was known for his skills as a physician. In the 1530s, after his wife and children died from the plague, the grief-stricken Nostradamus abandoned the medical profession to develop his gift of prophecy. In one early notable incident, Nostradamus bowed before a humble monk who was walking down the road and addressed

The French oracle Nostradamus is credited with predicting historical events hundreds of years before they actually happened.

him as "Your Holiness," a title reserved for the pope. Fifty years later, that monk, Felice Peretti, became Pope Sixtus V—nineteen years after the death of the French oracle.

In 1555, Nostradamus began work on a collection of prophecies called *Centuries*. The ten short books, which are published today in one volume, consist of predictions about world events that would take place until the year 3797 when Nostradamus said the world would end.

Centuries is so titled because the predictions are organized in nine groups of 100, except for one set of 42. These 942 prophecies consist of four-line poems called quatrains. Like thousands of oracles before him, Nostradamus seems to have deliberately made his predictions cloudy and difficult to decipher. They were written in Latin, Greek, and Old French, a language that was antiquated even in the sixteenth century. In addition the oracle invented words and inserted anagrams, words formed by reordering the letters of another word or phrase.

Despite their deliberately evasive language, the words of Nostradamus have been connected to dozens of historical events that took place in the nearly 450 years since *Centuries* was written. Believers say the oracle predicted, among other things, the Great London Fire of 1666, the French Revolution in the late eighteenth century, and the rise of German dictator Adolf Hitler, which resulted in World War II. It is also said that he predicted rockets, described as "the devise of flying fire," and submarines, which he called "iron fish."

Did Nostradamus Predict September 11?

Nostradamus has also been credited with predicting events in the United States, a country that did not even exist in the sixteenth century. In recent years, Nostradamus has been credited with foreseeing the destruction of the Twin Towers of the World Trade Center by hijackers on September 11, 2001. To back this claim, believers single out the verses from Century 6, quatrains 97 and 98, as pertaining to the event:

At forty-five degrees the sky will burn,

Fire to approach the great new city:

In an instant a great scattered flame will leap up,

When one will want to demand proof from the Normans.

Ruin . . . so very terrible with fear,

Their great city stained, pestilential dead:

To plunder the Sun and Moon and to violate their temples:

And to redden the two rivers flowing with blood. [61]

While most of the verse is self-explanatory, believers say that New York City lies "near" forty-five degrees, at forty degrees latitude north, and that the "two rivers" could be the Hudson and East Rivers that flow around Manhattan. Skeptics point out, however, that New York is three hundred miles south of forty five degrees. They say Nostradamus was really writing about Villeneuve-sur-Lot in France—as Villeneuve means "new city"—which actually is located at forty-five degrees latitude. And the Normans, descendants of tenth-century Scandinavians, later ruled England. Their inclusion in this quatrain would have little to do with events on September 11.

Unfortunately, wildly inaccurate quotes said to be from Nostradamus began to circulate around the globe via e-mail in the hours and days after the terrorist attacks. The follow-

Some people believe that Nostradamus predicted the terrorist attacks of September 11, 2001.

Predicting the Rise of Hitler?

Those who believe in the accuracy of the predictions of Nostradamus say that his writings foretold a series of tyrannical leaders called anti-Christs. Some say that one of those anti-Christs was German dictator Adolf Hitler, whose invasion of Poland in 1939 triggered World War II. The relevant verses are analyzed by Will McWhorter on the Homepage of Will McWhorter:

The second anti-Christ Nostradamus [mentioned] was "a man stained with murder . . . the great enemy of the human race . . . one who was worse than any who had gone before . . . bloody and inhuman . . ." In some quatrains Nostradamus refers to Hitler as the child or sometimes captain of Germany. Here are two examples:

He shall come to tyrannize the land.
He shall raise up a hatred that had long been dormant. The child of Germany observes no law.
Cries, and tears, fire, blood, and battle.

A captain of Germany shall come to yield himself by false hope,
So that his revolt shall cause great bloodshed.

All of these images certainly describe . . . Hitler. . . . In the following verse, some experts say that Nostradamus actually referred to Hitler by name but missed by one letter.

Beasts wild with hunger will cross the rivers
The greater part of the battlefield will be against Hister.

Finally, Nostradamus sums up Hitler's life and even predicts the fact that his death in Berlin in 1945 would never be satisfactorily confirmed:

Near the Rhine from the Austrian mountains
Will be born a great man of the people, come too late.
A man who will defend Poland and Hungary
And whose fate will never be certain.

ing six-line poem, which appeared on the *Urban Legends and Folklore* website, is a distortion of the "new city" quatrain:

Two steel birds will fall from the sky on the Metropolis.
The sky will burn at forty-five degrees latitude.
Fire approaches the great new city
Immediately a huge, scattered flame leaps up.
Within months, rivers will flow with blood.
The undead will roam earth for little time. [62]

This example is just one of many in which people have garbled the words of an already ambiguous oracle in order to claim that Nostradamus had accurately foreseen various tragedies in modern times.

The Mysterious Methods of Nostradamus

Although Nostradamus remains famous almost five centuries after his death, no one knows how he arrived at his forecasts. By any measure, the man was a genius, with a mastery of several languages, along with mathematics, medicine, astronomy, astrology, and other sciences of the day. He was also said to consult ancient texts on magic and sorcery to aid him in his predictions. These books contained magic spells, called invocations, that consisted of special sets of words or chants that were used to call up supernatural spirits for assistance in foretelling the future. The books also suggested magic charms to be used in spells that consisted of candles, oils, and special herbs. In *Nostradamus: The Man Who Saw Through Time*, a biographer describes the herbs in the oracle's work space:

> About the study clung the dry, pungent odors of blended herbs, of which a few clusters were visible. The rest, powdered or distilled for use [in magic spells], filled a variety of earthenware jars. Sometimes a fresher fragrance gave its odor to the room. This was when [his wife] Anne Nostradamus would climb the steep flights of narrow stairs to bring a jar of roses . . . from her garden. [63]

Nostradamus combined his herb-induced incantations with what is said to have been a natural gift of clairvoyance—that is, the power to see objects or events that cannot be perceived by the senses.

Clairvoyance

In the centuries since Nostradamus prognosticated in his chambers, many oracles have claimed to use clairvoyance as their main means of divination. The states of clairvoyance are often achieved through hypnotism or trances. For example, Andrew Jackson Davis rose to fame in 1845 when he foretold the future while in a trancelike state that he called "magnetic sleep," achieved through hypnotism. Davis made a name for himself when he published divinatory books that he dictated to Reverend William Fishbough. Davis delivered some of his prognostications in fluent Hebrew, a language the oracle did not study, know, or understand in his normal mental state.

Among his early achievements, Davis predicted that there were nine planets in the solar system instead of the seven

American clairvoyant Andrew Jackson Davis foretold the future through hypnotism.

Dream of Disaster

While many oracles are professionals, some people have one-time dreams of prophecy that inexplicably are borne out by events. One of the most studied cases comes from a calamity that occurred on October 21, 1966, in the little mining town of Aberfan, Wales. On that day, at 9:15 A.M. the village was buried under an avalanche of half a million tons of coal waste that had been piled on a hill high above the town. The mountain of coal waste killed 116 children and 28 adults when it buried an elementary school and other buildings.

After the disaster, reports of premonitory dreams began to fill newspapers. Some of these were described by Preston E. Dennett on the *Atlantis Rising* website:

> One lady had a nightmare that she suffocated in "deep blackness." Another dreamed of a small child being buried by a large landslide. Another clearly saw a schoolhouse be buried by an avalanche of coal, and rescue workers digging frantically for survivors. Another woke up from a nightmare in which she was being buried alive.

> On the morning of the disaster, [one woman] woke from a dream in which she saw children being overcome by "a black, billowing mass."

Probably the clearest of the premonitions was reported by a man in northwestern England who claimed that the night before the disaster, he had a dream which consisted only of letters being spelled out in dazzling light, A-B-E-R-F-A-N. At the time, the dream had no meaning to him. Hours later, he would realize with horror what it meant.

Several people reported having premonitory dreams shortly after the 1966 mining disaster in Aberfan, Wales.

known at that time. The oracle also made astounding predictions of technological achievements concerning trains and automobiles that would not take place for decades. For example, Davis foresaw an age of high-speed rail travel at a time when there were no railroads west of the Mississippi River. He wrote about railroad cars that were "spacious saloons, almost portable dwellings, moving with such speed that perhaps there will be advertisements—'Through to California in four days!'" He also seemed to foresee the age of the automobile when he mentioned horseless carriages that were powered by an "admixture of aqueous and atmospheric gases . . . traveling at high speeds."[64]

Davis died in 1910, around the time that another oracle was rising to prominence: Like oracles from ancient times, Edgar Cayce was said to get his messages directly from God. Cayce was known as the "sleeping prophet" because he closed his eyes and went into a trance before making his predictions, claiming that he had no memory or understanding of his words when he awoke. In April 1929, Cayce was said to have predicted the October 1929 stock market crash that ushered in the Great Depression. He was also said to have predicted World War II eight years before it began.

While believers point to these predictions as proof of Cayce's powers, skeptics point out that millions of people could have foreseen the crash of the highly overvalued stock market by 1929 and that many contemporary analysts openly feared that certain political events would lead to World War II. In addition, dozens of his predictions have been wrong. For example, he claimed that everyone in China—which today remains a Communist country—would convert to Christianity in 1958. He also made the apocalyptic prediction that a massive earthquake around 2000 would cause California to fall into the ocean, flood Japan, and change the geography in Europe. His mixed record notwithstanding, however, Cayce was certainly prolific; when he died in 1945, he left fourteen thousand "readings" behind, now stored in a library at Cayce's Association for Research and Enlightenment in Virginia.

Gazing into a Crystal Ball

In the 1960s, Jeane Dixon foretold the assassination of President Kennedy and became famous. Dixon said that this vision came to her when she was praying before a candle in church in 1952. The White House appeared before her, along with the number 1960, the year Kennedy was elected. She saw a dark cloud spread over the number as a handsome man with blue eyes and thick brown hair appeared. An "inner voice" told her that the Democratic president elected in 1960 would meet a violent death through assassination. In 1956, Dixon's prediction appeared in *Parade* magazine. Three years later, Dixon reversed herself and wrongly predicted Kennedy would not be elected in 1960.

In June 1963, however, when Kennedy had only one more year to serve, Dixon reiterated: "I still see a large coffin being carried into the White House. This means that the President will meet death elsewhere and his body will be returned there for national mourning." [65]

Five months later, after the president had been shot, Dixon became a national celebrity. Every year, after Christmas and before New Year's Eve, Dixon made predictions for the coming year that appeared in national magazines. Almost all of these prognostications were wrong, however. For example, Dixon stated that the Soviet Union would beat the United States in the race to the moon and that World War III would soon begin. She predicted that a cure for cancer could be discovered in 1967. In 1997, Dixon incorrectly predicted that actor Alec Baldwin would become terribly ill and comedian Ellen DeGeneres would be arrested by the Secret Service when she crashed the presidential inauguration. Despite her spotty record, Dixon's advice was valued by politicians and presidents; the oracle acted as an adviser to President Ronald Reagan for several years, and the president even arranged his travel schedule around Dixon's predictions.

Dixon often used a crystal ball to help her foretell the future. This activity, called scrying, consists of gazing into a shiny stone, mirror, or crystal ball. Believers claim that if a person concentrates hard enough while scrying, he or she can clear the consciousness and foretell the future. Skeptics say that Dixon, who died in 1997, was wrong about 99 percent of the time and have even coined a term called the "Jeane

Dixon effect" for the way people remember predictions that come true and forget those that do not.

Hungry for Predictions

While skeptics have long questioned the pronouncements of oracles, the public remains hungry for dramatic predictions, even if they never come true. Every December the pages of respected magazines and cheap tabloids are filled with prognostications about everything from celebrity marriages and divorces to fluctuations of the stock market. When real catastrophes occur, such as the disaster at the World Trade Center, the Internet quickly fills with questionable claims that some oracle actually predicted the event days, weeks, months, or even centuries ago. In this way, what seems like a senseless tragedy can be dealt with as a foregone conclusion precipitated by mysterious forces beyond human control. If this helps people deal with their grief, it can be a harmless exercise. If it distracts from the true causes of the disaster, however, it can prevent people from taking actions to prevent such tragedies from recurring.

Perhaps someday scientists will invent a method of time travel that will allow people to see into the future. With the knowledge of time and space expanding every day, it may come sooner than expected. Until that day, however, many people are likely to continue to use astrology, tarot cards, palmistry, and the *I Ching*. Whether these fortune-telling devices allow people to glimpse the future—or simply help them to better understand their own lives—is a question that, for now, has no answer.

Notes

Introduction: Predicting the Future

1. Scott Cunningham, *The Art of Divination*. Freedom, CA: Crossing Press, 1993, p. 4.
2. Quoted in Leon Lederman, Brian Greene, and Paul Davies, "What Can Be Said About Time?" *New Analysis of Time*, January 29, 2002. www.iwaynet.
3. Albert Einstein, "Future," *The Quote Project*, April 9, 2003. www.quoteproject.
4. Quoted in Michael Gilleland, "Horace, Ode 1.11," *Odes of Horace*, www.merriam park.com.
5. Robert Todd Carroll, "Tarot Cards," The *Skeptic's Dictionary*, 2002. http://skep dic.com.

Chapter 1: Astrology

6. Angus Hall and Francis King, *Mysteries of Prediction*. London: Bloomsbury, 1991, p. 138.
7. Quoted in Jim Tester, *A History of Western Astrology*. Wolfeboro, NH: Boydell Press, 1987, p. 13.
8. Saffi Crawford and Geraldine Sullivan, *The Power of Birthdays, Stars, & Numbers*. New York: Ballantine, 1998, p. 12.
9. Crawford and Sullivan, *The Power of Birthdays*, p. 13.
10. Llewellyn George, *The New A to Z Horoscope Maker and Delineator*. St. Paul, MN: Llewellyn, 1987, p. 221.

11. Bart J. Bok and Lawrence E. Jerome, *Objections to Astrology*. Buffalo, NY: Prometheus Books, 1975.
12. Helen Gurley Brown, *Cosmopolitan's Guide to Fortune-Telling*. New York: Cosmopolitan, 1977, p. 261.
13. Quoted in Gilleland, "Horace."

Chapter 2: Palm Reading

14. "The Digby Roll Manuscript," MS Digby Roll IV. http://users.breathe mail.net.
15. Quoted in Hall and King, *Mysteries of Prediction*, pp. 60–61.
16. Quoted in Hall and King, *Mysteries of Prediction*, p. 61.
17. Robert Todd Carroll, "Palmistry or Chiromancy," *The Skeptic's Dictionary*, 2002. http://skepdic.com.
18. Sasha Fenton and Malcolm Wright, *Palmistry*. New York: Crescent, 1996, p. 7.
19. Jane Struthers, *Predicting Your Future: The Complete Book of Divination*. London: Collins & Brown, 1997, p. 131.
20. Struthers, *Predicting Your Future*, p. 132.
21. Kevin Martin, *The Complete Gypsy Fortune-Teller*. New York: G.P. Putnam's Sons, 1970, pp. 48–49.
22. Struthers, *Predicting Your Future*, p. 138.

23. Martin, *The Complete Gypsy Fortune-Teller,* p. 49.
24. Struthers, *Predicting Your Future,* p. 141.
25. Fenton, *Palmistry,* pp. 32–33.
26. Struthers, *Predicting Your Future,* pp. 142–43.
27. Aristotle, "Aristotle's Treatise on Palmistry," *Serena's Guide to Divination,* 2002. www.serenapowers.com.
28. Fenton, *Palmistry,* p. 69.
29. Cunningham, *The Art of Divination,* p. 123.
30. Stephen Karcher, *The Elements of the I Ching.* Dorset, England: Element, 1995, p. 6.

Chapter 3: Tarot Cards

31. Jonathan Dee, *An Illustrated Guide to the Tarot.* New York: D&S, 2000, p. 7.
32. Stuart Kaplan, *The Encyclopedia of the Tarot.* New York: U.S. Games Systems, 1978, p. 12.
33. Dee, *An Illustrated Guide to the Tarot,* p. 34.
34. Roberta Peters, *Elementary Tarot.* London: Caxton Editions, 2000, p. 31.
35. Dee, *An Illustrated Guide to the Tarot,* p. 102.
36. Joan Bunning, *Learning the Tarot.* York Beach, ME: Weiser, 1998, p. 11.
37. Bunning, *Learning the Tarot,* p. 12.
38. Bunning, *Learning the Tarot,* p. 13.
39. Dee, *An Illustrated Guide to the Tarot,* p. 45.
40. Bunning, *Learning the Tarot,* p. 56.
41. Peters, *Elementary Tarot,* p. 6.
42. Carroll, "Tarot Cards."

Chapter 4: The *I Ching*

43. Karcher, *The Elements of the I Ching,* p. 5.
44. Quoted in Brown, *Cosmopolitan's Guide to Fortune-Telling,* p. 123.
45. Hall and King, *Mysteries of Prediction,* p. 40.
46. Richard John Lynn, trans., *The Classic of Changes.* New York: Columbia University Press, 1994, p. 205.
47. Richard Williams, ed., *Charting the Future.* Pleasantville, NY: Dorling Kindersley, 1992, p. 95.
48. Lynn, *The Classic of Changes,* p. 300.
49. Karcher, *The Elements of the I Ching,* p. 90.
50. Williams, *Charting the Future,* p. 97.
51. Lynn, *The Classic of Changes,* p. 200.
52. Lynn, *The Classic of Changes,* p. 202.
53. Quoted in Lynn, *The Classic of Changes,* pp. 28–29.
54. Karcher, *The Elements of the I Ching,* p. 9.
55. Robert Todd Carroll, "I Ching," *The Skeptic's Dictionary,* 2002. http://skepdic.com.
56. Karcher, *The Elements of the I Ching,* p. 7.

Chapter 5: Oracles

57. Herbert B. Greenhouse, *Premonitions: A Leap into the Future.* New York: Bernard Geis, 1971, p. 133.
58. Quoted in Justine Glass, *They Foresaw the Future.* New York: G.P. Putnam's Sons, 1969, p. 42.
59. Glass, *They Foresaw the Future,* p. 39.

60. Quoted in Glass, *They Foresaw the Future*, p. 40.

61. Quoted in Edgar Leoni, *Nostradamus and His Prophecies*, New York: Bell, 1982, p. 309.

62. David Emery, "Rumor Watch: Terrorist Attack on U.S.," *Urban Legends and Folklore*, 2003. http://urbanlegends.about.com.

63. Lee McCann, *Nostradamus: The Man Who Saw Through Time*. New York: Wing, 1992, p. 140.

64. Quoted in Russell B. Adams, Jr., *Visions and Prophecies*. Alexandria, VA: Time-Life, 1989, p. 23.

65. Quoted in Ruth Montgomery, *A Gift of Prophesy: The Phenomenal Jeane Dixon*. New York: William Morrow, 1965, p. 7.

For Further Reading

Books

Page Bryant, *Star Magic*. Jackson, TN: Dragonhawk, 2002. Information for young adults about and the history of Wiccan magic, astrology, and shamanistic belief.

Carl R. Green and William R. Sanford, *Fortune Telling*. Hillside, NJ: Enslow, 1993. Various methods of divination explained along with skeptical inquiries about their accuracy.

Gillian Kemp, *Tea Leaves, Herbs, and Flowers: Fortune Telling the Gypsy Way!* London: HarperCollins UK, 1998. An exploration of divinatory methods traditionally used by eastern European fortune-tellers.

Janina Renée, *Tarot for a New Generation*. St. Paul, MN: Llewellyn, 2001. This book, written for young adults, is a practical guidebook to the tarot that explains the history, how to perform a reading, the meaning of each card, and how the cards interact with one another.

Alvin Schwartz, *Telling Fortunes: Love Magic, Dream Signs, and Other Ways to Learn the Future*. New York: Lippincott, 1987. A collection of traditional beliefs, popular sayings, and superstitions that can be used as games to determine the future.

Internet Sources

Aubrey, "Tarot Court Card Readings." www.iol.ie/~aubrey/court.htm. A web page with the four suits of the page, knight, queen, and king cards from the tarot deck along with an explanation of their various meanings.

Facade, "I Ching," 2003. www.facade.com. A web page with links to *I Ching* readings for dozens of celebrities, including Moby, Mariah Carey, and Christina Aguilera.

Facade, "Today's Tarot," 2003. www.facade.com. A web page with links to tarot readings for dozens of celebrities.

Works Consulted

Books

Russell B. Adams, Jr., *Visions and Prophecies.* Alexandria, VA: Time-Life, 1989. An illustrated history of divination covering subjects from clairvoyance to palmistry.

Mir Bashir, *Your Past, Your Present and Your Future Through the Art of Hand Analysis.* Garden City, NY: Doubleday, 1974. A guide to palmistry with several separate chapters concerning skin texture, finger types, palm features, and lines in the hand.

Bart J. Bok and Lawrence E. Jerome, *Objections to Astrology.* Buffalo, NY: Prometheus Books, 1975. A book endorsed by 192 of the world's leading scientists that offers a full range of criticisms of the theories behind astrological divination.

Helen Gurley Brown, *Cosmopolitan's Guide to Fortune-Telling.* New York: Cosmopolitan Books, 1977. A comprehensive guide to tea leaf reading, numerology, the *I Ching,* clairvoyance, astrology, and other divinatory systems written for female readers of *Cosmopolitan* magazine.

Joan Bunning, *Learning the Tarot.* York Beach, ME: Weiser, 1998. A how-to book with a lesson format meant to teach beginners basic and advanced concepts for reading the tarot.

Saffi Crawford and Geraldine Sullivan, *The Power of Birthdays, Stars, & Numbers.* New York: Ballantine, 1998. Two astrologers list 365 personality traits, career strengths, and tips on love for individual birthdays.

Scott Cunningham, *The Art of Divination.* Freedom, CA: Crossing Press, 1993. The exploration of dozens of divination methods, from crystal gazing to palmistry, written by an author who has penned dozens of books on New Age subject matter.

Jonathan Dee, *An Illustrated Guide to the Tarot.* New York: D&S, 2000. The history and symbolism of the seventy-eight-card tarot deck, with beautiful illustrations and interpretations of each card.

Sasha Fenton and Malcolm Wright, *Palmistry.* New York: Crescent, 1996. A book for palm readers with 285 illustrations that depict the lines, structure, and characteristics of the hand, along with what they mean.

Llewellyn George, *The New A to Z Horoscope Maker and Delineator.* St. Paul, MN: Llewellyn, 1987. A best-selling guide to astrology with detailed information that allows the reader to construct and interpret horoscopes.

Fred Gettings, *The Hand and the Horoscope.* London: Triune, 1973. A book that ties astrology to palmistry, joining the planets and signs of the zodiac to the fingers, palm, and other parts of the hand.

Justine Glass, *They Foresaw the Future.* New York: G.P. Putnam's Sons, 1969. A historic account of six thousand examples of prophecy, from ancient Egypt to well-known twentieth-century predictors such as Edgar Cayce and Jeane Dixon.

Herbert B. Greenhouse, *Premonitions: A Leap into the Future.* New York: Bernard Geis, 1971. The details of dozens of disasters, wars, and other major events that were foretold by amateur and professional oracles in premonitions.

Angus Hall and Francis King, *Mysteries of Prediction.* London: Bloomsbury, 1991. An examination of various divination practices and how they allegedly work.

Stuart Kaplan, *The Encyclopedia of the Tarot.* New York: U.S. Games Systems, 1978. An illustrated examination of hundreds of tarot decks with pictures and descriptions, written by an expert who owns the world's largest collection of tarot cards.

———, *Hanson-Roberts Tarot Deck.* New York: U.S. Games Systems, 1985. Descriptions and meanings of cards and instructions on how to use them, from a booklet included in the tarot deck illustrated by Mary Hanson-Roberts.

Stephen Karcher, *The Elements of the I Ching.* Dorset, England: Element, 1995. An examination of the roots and history of the ancient Chinese *Book of Changes,* with instructions on using the book to predict the future.

Edgar Leoni, *Nostradamus and His Prophecies.* New York: Bell, 1982. A biography of one of history's most famous oracles along with the complete version of his *Centuries* in both English and the original French.

Richard John Lynn, trans., *The Classic of Changes.* New York: Columbia University Press, 1994. An updated translation of the classic *I Ching* with commentary in English by Wang Bi, a Chinese scholar from the third century A.D.

Kevin Martin, *The Complete Gypsy Fortune-Teller.* New York: G.P. Putnam's Sons, 1970. A study of fortune-telling techniques traditionally practiced by Gypsies, including palmistry, cartomancy, tea leaf reading, and astrology.

Lee McCann, *Nostradamus: The Man Who Saw Through Time.* New York: Wing, 1992. First published in 1941, this is the biography of the sixteenth-century French oracle whose predictions are still discussed more than four centuries since his death.

Gary G. Melyan and Wen-kuang Chu, *I-Ching: The Hexagrams Revealed.* Rutland, VT: Charles E. Tuttle, 1977. A do-it-yourself divination guide with various interpretations of the hexagrams that make up the text of the *Book of Changes.*

Ruth Montgomery, *A Gift of Prophesy: The Phenomenal Jeane Dixon.* New York: William Morrow, 1965. A best-selling account of a woman whose predictions were sought by the public and presidents alike.

Joseph Murphy, *Secrets of the I Ching.* Paramus, NJ: Reward, 2000. A how-to guide to the

Chinese book of divination with lessons about and interpretations from the ancient text.

Roberta Peters, *Elementary Tarot*. London: Caxton Editions, 2000. The history of the tarot, meaning of the cards, and interpretations by an author with twenty-five years of experience in tarot reading.

Comte C. de Saint-Germain, *The Practice of Palmistry*. London: Newcastle, 1973. First published in 1897, this book is encyclopedic in scope and written as a guidebook for professional chiromancers.

Dianne Skafte, *Listening to the Oracle*. San Francisco: HarperSanFrancisco, 1997. An examination of oracles said to be found in nature, images, dreams, and elsewhere with a discussion as to how to find and utilize their wisdom to improve life.

Jane Struthers, *Predicting Your Future: The Complete Book of Divination*. London: Collins & Brown, 1997. A book about various methods for predicting the future written as a guide for readers who want to divine their own fortunes using the tarot, astrology, numerology, and palmistry.

Jim Tester, *A History of Western Astrology*. Wolfeboro, NH: Boydell Press, 1987. A scholarly text pertaining to the roots of modern astrological prediction in ancient Mesopotamia and Greece, the Middle Ages in the Middle East, and the Renaissance period in Europe.

Arlene Tognetti and Lisa Lenard, *The Complete Idiot's Guide to Tarot and Fortune-Telling*. New York: Alpha, 1999. An exploration of the tarot deck written for amateur cartomancers who want to find out about love, life, and their destinies.

Richard Williams, ed., *Charting the Future*. Pleasantville, NY: Dorling Kindersley, 1992. An illustrated exploration of astrology, the *I Ching*, palmistry, tarot cards, and other methods of divining the future.

Internet Sources

Aristotle, "Aristotle's Treatise on Palmistry," *Serena's Guide to Divination*, 2002. www.serenapowers.com. A guide to palm reading allegedly written by the famous Greek philosopher in 335 B.C. and printed in Great Britain in 1738.

Robert Todd Carroll, "I Ching," *The Skeptic's Dictionary*, 2002. http://skepdic.com. A web page by a skeptic of supernatural beliefs with the history and workings of the ancient Chinese *Book of Changes* and criticism for those who believe in such methods of divination.

———, "Palmistry or Chiromancy," *The Skeptic's Dictionary*, 2002. http://skepdic.com. The history and practice of palmistry by a writer who has remained unpersuaded of the worth of the practice.

———, "Tarot Cards," *The Skeptic's Dictionary*, 2002. http://skepdic.com. A page on the history and basic workings of the tarot deck with questions as to how or why these cards can predict the future.

Preston E. Dennett, "Premonitions of Disaster," *Atlantis Rising*, 1996–2002. www.atlantisrising.com. An investigation into the validity of premonitions of famous disasters throughout the twentieth century.

Albert Einstein, "Future," *The Quote Project,* April 9, 2003. www.quoteproject.com. A site with dozens of quotes about the future by famous authors, scholars, actors, politicians, and others.

David Emery, "Rumor Watch: Terrorist Attack on U.S.," *Urban Legends and Folklore,* 2003. http://urbanlegends.about. com. A web page challenging poems that circulated on the Internet concerning the terrorist attack on the World Trade Center that have been wrongly attributed to Nostradamus.

Michael Gilleland, "Horace, Ode 1.11," *Odes of Horace.* www.merriampark.com. A site with lines from poems concerning divination written by the ancient Roman poet Horace.

"The Digby Roll Manuscript." http://users. breathemail.net. The text from the first book written on palmistry, in 1440, from the original manuscript kept at Oxford College in England.

Leon Lederman, Brian Greene, and Paul Davies, "What Can Be Said About Time?" *New Analysis of Time,* January 29, 2002. www.iwaynet.net. A site with quotes and theories concerning the nature of time by those who study physics.

Tom Tadfor Little, "The Hermitage, a Tarot History Site," *The Hermitage,* 1999–2001. www.tarothermit.com. A site with a brief history of the tarot deck that includes links to more than a dozen other sites concerning theories, origins, games, and cards in the deck.

Will McWhorter, "Nostradamus: Predictions for the Past, Present and Future," *Homepage of Will McWhorter,* April 29, 1993. http://boisdarc.tamucommerce.edu. A site with extensive analysis of the writings of Nostradamus and his predictions as they relate to historical events of the last five hundred years.

James Randi, "Commentary," *James Randi Educational Foundation,* June 15, 2001. http://www.randi.org. A web page with commentary about the failure of astrology to predict the slaughter of Nepal's royal family by Crown Prince Dipendra in June 2001.

Index

Picture Credits

About the Author

Stuart A. Kallen is the author of more than 150 nonfiction books for children and young adults. He has written on topics ranging from the theory of relativity to the history of rock and roll. In addition, Mr. Kallen has written award-winning children's videos and television scripts. In his spare time, Stuart A. Kallen is a singer/songwriter/guitarist in San Diego, California.